SMOKING HOT & COLD

TECHNIQUES AND RECIPES FOR SMOKED MEAT, SEAFOOD, DAIRY, AND VEGETABLES

CHARLOTTE PIKE

Charlotte Pike is the author of *Fermented* (2015), which was shortlisted for an André Simon Award, and *The Hungry Student Cookbook* series (2013), which won an International Gourmand Award. A graduate of the Ballymaloe Certificate Course, Charlotte has contributed to many cookbooks and publications by writing recipes and food styling and occasionally reports on food for BBC Radio.

As a deeply passionate advocate of good food, Charlotte spends much of her time traveling the world learning about and searching for the best food and drink, and recreating recipes in her kitchen.

PHOTOGRAPHY BY TARA FISHER

KYLE BOOKS

FOR MY PARENTS, WITH LOVE AND THANKS

Published in 2017 by Kyle Books
www.kylebooks.com

Distributed by National Book Network
4501 Forbes Blvd, Suite 200,
Lanham, MD 20706
Phone: (800) 462-6420
Fax: (800) 338-4550
customercare@nbnbooks.com

First published in Great Britain in 2017 by Kyle Books
an imprint of Kyle Cathie Limited

10 9 8 7 6 5 4 3 2 1

ISBN 978-1-909487-68-0

Library of Congress Control Number: 2017940453

Editor: **Vicky Orchard**
Design: **Lucy Gowans**
Photography: **Tara Fisher**
Food styling: **Annie Rigg**
Props styling: **Tabitha Hawkins**
Production: **Nic Jones and Gemma John**
Proofreader: **Jane Bamforth**
Editorial adaptation: **Christy Lusiak**

Color reproduction by ALTA, London
Printed and bound in China by 1010 International Printing Ltd.

CONTENTS

INTRODUCTION   4

FISH   14

DAIRY   60

MEAT   78

VEGETABLES & SALT   118

INDEX   142

INTRODUCTION

Smoking is an ancient and delicious art and has to be one of the most magical ways of cooking food. There is something so deeply satisfying about cooking in such a comparatively primitive way by modern standards, and you are rewarded with the most mouthwatering results. Most people find the smell of wood smoke alone incredibly evocative and comforting. It's instinctive, reassuring, and primeval—after all, fire has always signified warmth, the comfort of home, the preparation of food, and, perhaps, most crucially, survival.

It is much easier and quicker to smoke your own food than most people think. There are endless opportunities for creativity with a great number of ingredients and combinations of flavors of wood, whose aromas can be incorporated. Little is required in terms of equipment and space, and there are many pieces of portable equipment available. If you don't have an outside patio, you can smoke on the stovetop in the kitchen, or even take a portable smoker to the beach or on a picnic or fishing trip. Building your own smoker is an option but only if you feel so inclined, as there are many excellent ready-to-go smokers on the market at a range of prices. To start to smoke your own food is to embark on a never-ending adventure.

Smoking is a method of flavoring, cooking, and extending the life of food and has been used in many cultures all over the world for thousands of years. Traditionally, ingredients—predominantly meat and fish—were salted, dried, and then smoked, so they could subsequently be kept for the short term, extending the availability of valuable protein in the diet during lean months but, unlike salting, drying, or fermenting, smoke is not a long-term preservative. There is evidence of smoking used by ancient civilizations, such as fish smoking in Mesopotamia in 3500 BC; there are remains of a smokehouse on the River Bann in Northern Ireland dating back to 2000 BC, and of black smoked apricots in the Chinese Tang dynasty (AD 618–907). Nowadays, smoking is mainly undertaken for flavor, rather than preservation. The flavor of smoke ranges from a subtle and delicious extra dimension to robust, woody notes added to an ingredient.

Wood smoke contains hundreds of components that coat the exposed surfaces and gently penetrate an ingredient, creating an impermeable tarry outer layer, which lightly seals the ingredient and acts as a barrier to pests and bacteria. The longer the ingredient is smoked for, the more the flavor penetrates and the stronger the flavor of the smoke.

WAYS OF SMOKING

There are two methods of smoking; hot smoking and cold smoking. Many of us are most familiar with cold-smoked ingredients, such as traditional smoked salmon and smoked bacon.

Hot smoking takes place generally between 140 and 220°F and either fully or partially cooks an ingredient. The smoky flavor is imparted and the food is lightly cooked. It is the quickest and, generally speaking, easiest way to smoke food. Meat will often need further cooking once it has been smoked, to make it safe or more palatable and to improve the texture—crisping the skin on a duck breast, rendering fat on any cut, or achieving sizzling skins on sausages. Some fish and shellfish will be adequately cooked through once they are hot smoked and can be served immediately.

Cold smoking takes place between 50 and 85°F, although often at 85°F. This method is used to saturate the ingredient in smoke, but not to cook it. Cold smoking very gently dries out the food and imparts a smoky flavor. It is a process that has traditionally been undertaken in the fall months—as the ambient temperature must not exceed the temperature at which you are smoking or you'll run into problems.

Apart from hardwoods (never use softwoods), such as oak, apple, beech, maple, and hickory chips, there are many materials that can be used to generate smoke, and they include charcoal, tea, seaweed, hay, peat, rice, or sugar. This is where you can play. You can make up your own mixes and store them in jars, using two tablespoons at a time, whenever you smoke food. These mixes will keep well, stored in an airtight container or lidded Mason jar. Try mixing ¾ cup tea leaves, seaweed, or hay with ¼ cup white rice and ¼ cup sugar. Shake to mix well, and put this dry mix straight in the smoker. This mix will not start to take as quickly as wood, so be patient. You can smoke using whichever material you like for as long as you like (accepting the added pungency in flavor). The smoking times can be varied to suit your tastes.

The real joy of smoking is that there are very few concrete rules to follow. You will find your way as you go and very soon you will be able to tailor your smoking to suit your personal tastes. Whatever you produce will taste totally unique and quite unlike commercially produced versions. It can be difficult to give very specific instructions as to what to do, as the processes vary significantly depending on ingredients, climate, and equipment, but you should quickly get a feel for what works for you and what you like. Make sure to record your experiments, and enjoy the process.

I'd recommend starting with shorter smokes to enable you to monitor the smoker, how it performs, and the signs of what to look for first, rather than embarking on a long smoke at the beginning.

There are many more ingredients that can be smoked than are in this book. The recipes that are included are some of the most delicious and useful to try, and they work extremely well in so many recipes. But once you have mastered your techniques, the world is your oyster. You'll need to invest a little time and acquire a couple of pieces of equipment, but the rewards for your investment are truly exciting. Let's get started.

HOW TO PREPARE YOUR INGREDIENTS FOR SMOKING

The first rule is this: if you are smoking a raw ingredient in its original state, such as a fillet of fish, a vegetable, or a cut of meat, then it will need salting, curing, or brining before it is smoked. You need to allow time for this presmoking stage, and then for essential drying once your ingredient has been prepared.

If you are smoking an ingredient that has already undergone some kind of preparation, then it is ready to smoke. This includes cheese, butter, and processed meats such as sausages.

Each ingredient will need to be dried thoroughly beforehand, and that can be done simply by patting with paper towels to ensure it's fully dry. This allows the smoke to stick to the surface and penetrate the ingredient and creates a pellicle—a very lightly sticky, but not wet, surface, onto which the smoke attaches itself.

SALTING

Salting is the most basic way of preparing your ingredients for smoking, to flavor and draw out the moisture. This works best with vegetables, seafood, and small fillets of fish or meat. All you need to do is sprinkle them with sea salt and leave them, covered, in the fridge for 2 hours before drying the ingredients and putting them into either a hot or a cold smoker. If you feel an ingredient might be too salty once it's rested in the fridge, then wash it by rinsing it under cold water and dry fully before smoking.

Traditional salting—where an ingredient is entirely covered in salt to form a crust and left to salt for several days before being rinsed, dried, and smoked—is not required for these recipes with the exception of the bacon recipe (see page 80) because it is very important to draw as much water as possible from the meat. For that I like to use sea salt, which is completely pure and free from anticaking agents, but it can be quite expensive when so much salt is required, so do look for pure salt, sold in large bags. Some supermarkets and fishmongers sell them, and they can be sourced online.

CURING

Curing draws moisture from the ingredient, which promotes the absorption of smoke and also inhibits the growth of bacteria, which thrive in a moist environment.

Dry curing is done by rubbing a dry mix of salt and sugar into the ingredient, usually meat or fish. The mix can be customized to include spices and herbs. A basic dry cure could be made using ⅓ cup sea salt and 2½ tablespoons sugar, but you can increase this to half sugar, half salt for a sweeter cure. This amount will cure approximately 2¼ pounds meat, and can be increased or decreased accordingly, depending on how much of the ingredient you wish to cure. Simply stir the sugar and salt together. Place the ingredient in a large, shallow-sided dish and sprinkle with the cure, rubbing it into the flesh on all sides, and then cover the dish and set aside to cure in the fridge. You may need to drain the dish regularly, as meat will release liquid as it cures. Alternatively, you can sit your meat on a rack—which could be as simple as an old cooling rack or even a piece of chicken wire cut to size.

Cure your ingredient for as long as you wish—personal taste, the size of the cut, and the ambient temperature will influence this. Thick cuts will take longer to cure than thin, and also the curing process will take much less time in warmer weather, as opposed to cold. Fish cures more quickly than meat. The thickness and density can also affect the speed of curing—thick and dense ingredients take longer. A general rule would be 2 to 6 hours, but it can be as little as 30 minutes or as much as 5 days.

Once your ingredient is cured, it should generally be rinsed in cold, fresh water and fully dried before smoking. This is to remove any impurities if they have been extracted from the meat.

BRINING

Brining before smoking works with any ingredient you wish to smoke. It is a quicker method of preparing your ingredient than traditional salting. This makes it a good technique for larger quantities, such as a big cut of beef or venison, a whole side of salmon, or a large bird. Brine is a solution of pure salt dissolved in fresh water. If your tap water isn't very pure, then do consider spring or mineral water as an alternative. As with any of the presmoking processes, you can adjust the length of time you prepare the ingredient for: generally 48 hours is enough for a large cut of meat, 12 to 24 hours for a fillet of salmon. Select an appropriate-sized container—I use a large glass or ceramic mixing bowl or a large, scrupulously clean plastic container or bucket. It needs to be big enough to ensure that the ingredient is fully submerged and, if you are brining more than one piece at a time, that ingredients are not touching. Never brine different ingredients together in the same container.

To thoroughly clean the containers used for these processes, put them in the dishwasher on the hottest setting or wash and rinse completely with boiling water to sterilize.

A simple brine can be made by dissolving 3 cups salt in 3 quarts of cold, fresh water. If you find this too salty, reduce the amount of salt to 2 cups.

If you are brining for more than 24 hours, stir the brine to encourage any undissolved salt to distribute. It is generally not considered safe to reuse brine, so after it has been used once, discard it.

DRYING

It is essential for your ingredient to be properly dry before it is smoked. Use your judgment here: it may be sufficient to pat it dry with a clean cloth or paper towels. If, however, your ingredient feels really wet and perhaps a little slimy, even after carefully drying it with a cloth, you will need to either rest it on a plate or hang it up to dry fully before using it. For recipes such as bacon and cold-smoked salmon, hang the ingredient to dry for at least 12 hours in a fridge. Traditionally this would have been done in a larder or meat locker.

To monitor the temperature, it's best to buy a smoker with a thermometer for reading the ambient temperature inside the smoker, rather than sticking a meat thermometer into the ingredient, although of course you can do this too.

Left: Glazing Asian-Spiced Smoked Beef Ribs (page 111) on the Big Green Egg as they smoke.

RUBS AND MARINADES

For another layer of flavor to your hot smokes, try adding a rub to the ingredient when you are salting it. Make up a dry mix and rub it into the meat, leaving it for at least an hour before smoking. Try making your own mixes using dried spices and herbs. You can use anything from black pepper, red pepper flakes, cinnamon, cloves, nutmeg, caraway, cumin, fennel seeds, oregano, rosemary, thyme, and mustard in the form of ground spices, crushed seeds, or premade mixes. Ensure the sea salt is mixed in, and a little sugar, too, if you would like some sweetness. You'll need about ½ cup of a rub to cover a few steaks or chicken breasts, and this could be made up with 2 tablespoons of salt, 2 tablespoons of sugar, and 2 tablespoons each of, say, cumin and thyme.

Marinades are another way of adding flavor. They mostly contain oil—perhaps olive, sunflower, or sesame—an acid, such as citrus fruit juice or a wine vinegar and some flavorings, which might include garlic, ginger, red pepper flakes, citrus rind, and fresh herbs. Again, ½ cup will probably be enough here, so why not try 3 tablespoons of oil, 3 tablespoons of citrus juice, such as fresh lemon juice, and 2 tablespoons of chopped herbs and garlic. Again, you can marinate for at least an hour before smoking, but longer, or even overnight, will work fine—it will just intensify the flavor.

The quantities you make for rubs and marinades can be multiplied or divided to suit the amount of food you are smoking in one batch.

EQUIPMENT

Equipment might seem like a barrier to embarking on home smoking. The good news is that you don't need to be a DIY enthusiast, nor do you require much specialty equipment or space to get smoking, and there are options for every budget. Feel free to get creative and make your own hot and cold smokers if you are so inclined.

HOT SMOKERS

My go-to smoker is my Big Green Egg (see below left), which I keep outside and use to both grill and smoke. I have one in a large size, which is enormous, but has plenty of room to smoke whole fish and large cuts of meat, such as legs of lamb, on the grill rack. I also have a small one, which is portable, and useful for keeping in the back of the car and taking out to the beach or countryside to smoke on. They are easy to use, require hardly any cleaning, and stay at the correct temperature for hours.

Other lidded barbecue grills can perform a secondary function as a smoker, so if you already have one, it is worth checking the specifications of the model, as you may well be able to use it. Using a grill to smoke does not prevent you from using it as a grill, too. It should have a lid that seals so that it can smoke.

For a more hi-tech experience, professional smokers such as Bradley and Cookshack are an option. They are expensive, but can be relied on, which is particularly helpful for smoking very regularly or if consistency is required for catering or other purposes. That said, it is perfectly possible to smoke regularly and consistently using other methods.

If you're after a useful smaller piece of equipment, then a Camerons stovetop smoker (page 24) works well. It is made of stainless steel and is especially good for smoking fish and vegetables, although larger pieces of meat will not fit into the tray. It is very versatile and can be used indoors on gas and electric stoves, and outdoors on an electric or gas grill.

A good portable hot smoker is the Abu Garcia smoker (see below right), which is also stainless steel. The large sized one is big enough for smoking fish. It is completely portable and fueled by two small burners that run on denatured alcohol and sawdust. It is perfect for smoking fresh fish on a beach, boat, or camping trip.

For those who would prefer a dedicated smoker or are more creatively minded, it can be really fun to build your own custom smoker. If you are into upcycling, it can be a great way to create a completely unique piece of equipment, which can be made from all types of metal ware, such as lockers, barrels, and filing cabinets—I've even heard of old boilers being used. And if space is limited, you can make a stovetop smoker using a wok or even a deep metal pan, which is specially reserved for smoking. Line it with foil, place the chips in the bottom, and sit a rack on top. Sit the food on top of the rack and add a well-fitting lid.

COLD SMOKERS

If you want to try constructing your own smoker, then building a cold smoker is the most worthwhile task. Since the heat needs to be

Far left: Hot smoking garlic and onions on the Big Green Egg. Smoke is escaping from the chamber as the lid is opened.
Left: Abu Garcia hot smoker, clockwise from left: the unit with rack set in it, denatured alcohol and sawdust to light and smoke, and the tray with burners.

kept separate from the foods you are smoking, you'll need two chambers connected by a hose. A simple way to do this is to take a garden incinerator, drill or cut out a large hole, and affix a thermo conductive metal hose to the side, which connects to a secondary chamber, which might be a metal can, barrel, or wooden box, which is where your food will sit or hang. The possibilities are endless.

WOOD AND CHARCOAL

I have already touched on this, but it is essential to use only pure hardwood, which is designated for smoking purposes only and has had no artificial ingredients added. Planks, chips, chunks, and sawdust may be used, so long as they are pure wood.

Charcoal must be 100 percent pure and natural. I like the flavor of the Big Green Egg charcoal, which is a mixture of oak and hickory.

There are ever-increasing numbers of independent charcoal producers in operation, and I urge you to look locally for a company.

Right: Sawdust for an Abu Garcia smoker (top left); Big Green Egg charcoal (top right); long matches (middle); Big Green Egg lighter squares (middle right); large cherry wood chips for an outdoor hot smoker (bottom left); and fine oak chips for a stovetop smoker (bottom right).
Below left: The cold smoking chamber is ready to use when the smoke flows freely from the vent.

Many charcoals from small, independent producers have superior burning qualities, making them easy to light without the use of lighting fluid or fuel.

EXTRA EQUIPMENT

Some tongs, a spatula or two, a carving fork, some string, metal skewers, and scissors will get you started. It can also be useful to have some butcher's hooks for hanging meat and an electric thermometer to check internal temperatures of meat. A Thermapen thermometer is an excellent gadget to have in the kitchen, not just for smoking. When cold smoking dairy ingredients, I like to sit them in a shallow, nonmetallic, heatproof dish, as they can become a bit soft and melty around the edges as they smoke.

HOW TO BUILD A COLD SMOKER

What do you need?

- A galvanized/stainless steel trash can (ideally with galvanized/stainless steel lid)
- 4-inch diameter duct takeoff and collar (should come with nuts and bolts for mounting)
- Vent cap
- 4 x 20-inch stainless steel rods
- A 16-foot long (at least) piece of 4-inch diameter aluminum flexible duct (the longer you make this the lower the temperature in your cold smoker)
- A galvanized/stainless steel incinerator
- 2 x 4½-inch hose clamps (which will fit and seal around the ends of the aluminum ducting)
- Grill racks or similar

Above: Homemade cold smoker.

A note on trash cans and incinerators: the can and incinerator need to have lids that will fit onto each other. The tighter fitting the lids, the better, as you want to minimize the gap for air to escape through when the lid is fitted, as this will allow smoke to escape. In extreme cases it could cause the smoke to simply pour out of the top of your incinerator, rather than making it through to the cold-smoker!

If you don't like the idea of using trash cans, something similar can be constructed using two kettle grills, although the method differs slightly.

Equipment

- Safety glasses
- Protective/gardening gloves
- Marker pen
- Drill
- Metal snips
- Dremel angle grinder—will help neaten up and remove sharp edges (optional)

- Pliers
- 2 x large cans (I use 102-oz. tomato cans washed out with the lids removed.)

Health and safety

While making this smoker please ensure you wear appropriate protective equipment. As a minimum this should include safety glasses and sturdy gloves (either cut-proof, or gardening gloves, and ideally long-sleeved tops). Eye protection is crucial. Also please remember that the cuts you have made will leave sharp edges, so gloves and long-sleeve tops will dramatically reduce the risk of cuts and scrapes.

How to do it

Start with the trash can, which will be your smoking chamber. Take your duct takeoff and collar and draw around the outside of the 4-inch duct connector using a pen. It needs to be positioned at the base of the can, as this will allow the smoke to rise back up through it.

Next, cut out the hole you have drawn. You may need to use a drill to make some holes around the circle to start you off, then you can use metal snips to cut out the circle (you can also use pliers to fold over sharp edges, or soften them with a Dremel angle grinder).

Slide the 4-inch duct takeoff through the hole you have made so that the collar is inside the can, then mark and drill the holes for mounting it, and bolt into place. To get a good seal you'll need to really tighten the bolts; this will make the collar conform to the shape of the can.

Next, make a hole in the top of the can lid to allow the smoke to escape. First snip through the center of the handle and bend the remnants out of the way. Then take the vent cap and sit it in the center (top) of the can lid, in between the cut handle pieces. Draw a circle around the base of this vent, then draw a second circle inside this one, about 1 inch smaller in diameter. Cut this second circle out, as before.

You can modify the handle to hold on the vent cap. Use the metal snips to shorten the can lid handle to about 2¼ inches on each side. These can then be bent into shape to hold on your vent cap. Place the vent cap between the cut handle pieces to cover the hole and adjust as necessary. If you do this right it should be possible to lift up the lid by the vent, to give you an idea of how firmly it should sit in place. This allows smoke to flow out of the cold smoker and prevents rain or bugs from entering the chamber.

The smoking chamber is nearly complete. All you need to do now is drill some holes in the sides to feed your stainless steel rods through from one side to the other. I put two rods, widely spaced at the same height to hold up each rack. I also suggest putting a 90° bend about 2 inches from the end of each rod to help hold them in position. Add as many or as few as you like, in a variety of positions. I like to drill holes at the top of the can and feed the rods through there.

You can hang ingredients off the rods using metal hooks, or thread some string through and tie them up to hang. Or, you can sit a rack on top of the rods, and sit ingredients flat or set a dish on the rack, as it should be reasonably stable.

Place the aluminum ducting over the funnel on the lid of the incinerator and fasten tightly with a hose clamp. Then simply connect the other end of the hose, again fastening with a hose clamp, to the bottom of the can, affixing the pipe around the ring. Ensure the aluminum ducting is stretched out to its maximum length, as the length is crucial to shed heat from the smoke before it enters the smoking chamber (trash can).

Always light the fire in the incinerator chamber. Set one metal can upside down (base facing up) in the center of the bottom of the incinerator. Then put the second can on top of the first can, cut-side up, so you can place the charcoal into this can. It works better if elevated. Fill the top can with charcoal and light. The smoke will take off quickly, and you can start smoking your ingredients as soon as the smoke travels to the smoking chamber. The ingredients are set apart from the heat source, which means that there is no need to wait for it to cool down before smoking.

As hot air rises it is crucial that the smoking chamber (can) is elevated above the incinerator, so it is a good idea to set it on a bench or table (see photo opposite)—it can even be waist high—as long as it is stable.

For longer smokes, you may need to keep adding more charcoal and relighting to keep the smoke flowing. Just keep an eye on your smoker and see how it goes.

HOW TO SMOKE

HOT SMOKING

Hot smoking takes place between 140 and 220°F. You can go up to 240°F, but I find that ingredients can dry out significantly if the temperature rises above 200°F. The heat source is in the same chamber as the ingredient.

STOVETOP HOT SMOKER

The stovetop hot smoker is prepared as follows. Place 1½ to 2 tablespoons of small wood chips into the center of the base of your stovetop smoker. Set the drip tray on top of this (or cover with a large sheet of foil), and place the rack on top. Your prepared ingredients can now be put on the rack. Place the lid loosely on top, or slide the lid on, so that it is only just open. Set the smoker over the highest heat on the stove. You can also place the hot smoker on a hot barbecue or wood fire outdoors. When smoke starts to appear—just a few wisps at first—close the lid fully (use a cloth—it is surprisingly easy to burn yourself doing this) and reduce the heat to the stove's lowest setting before leaving to smoke. Check how your ingredients are progressing after the minimum cooking time is up. You may want to keep going until the color changes and the ingredient is cooked through, or you may want to achieve a very light smoke. To continue smoking, close the lid and keep the smoker on the lowest heat.

OUTDOOR HOT SMOKER

Fill the chamber with charcoal—about two-thirds full, but check instructions if you are using a bought smoker or grill—and place 1 to 3 handfuls of wood chips on the top, if you are using them. Light the smoker using a chemical-free lighter, and allow the fire to take, leaving the lid open and allowing the air to flow through. This should take about 10 minutes. When the fire takes, let it burn—or use the fire to grill—until it dies down and your smoker reaches the correct temperature—when it gets to 220°F you should be good to go as the temperature will start to drop from this point. Do use a thermometer to monitor the temperature. Your ingredient should be smoked before the fire dies out, but if the temperature really drops, you may need to stoke or relight the fire. Adding plenty of fuel (charcoal) at the start should help you achieve a long burn, but you will quickly get a feel for how your smoker works.

Another smoking option is to put a small foil tray of water into the smoker, which will lower the temperature in the smoker.

COLD SMOKING

Light your cold smoker in the same way as an outdoor hot smoker. I use a metal incinerator can as the heat source and inside I have two large, clean metal cans (see opposite). One is sat upside down on the base, and the second is placed the correct way up on top of that. The top can is filled with charcoal and wood chips and lit. As soon as the charcoal is lit, place the lid on and allow the smoke to start to generate. Set the smoking chamber higher than the heat source—either on a step or on a heatproof patio table or chair, as long as it is secure. Extend the piping as far as you can, which allows the smoke to cool as it travels into the smoking chamber.

HOW MUCH CAN YOU FIT IN A SMOKER AT A TIME?

It makes sense to fill your smoker if you are lighting it. Use all the space you can, but ensure that your ingredients are not touching or too crowded. If there is a chance of cross-contamination between ingredients, stack your smoker as you would your fridge: raw meat on the bottom, then cooked meat above, and dairy and vegetables placed on the very top. Put the ingredients directly on the racks unless the recipe specifies using a dish or other form of container. If there is a risk of dripping, then set your ingredients on shelves and place a pan, plate, or a sheet of foil underneath each ingredient to prevent it from dripping onto the next, but do ensure that the surface area of an ingredient is not covered or smoke prevented from flowing freely.

Homemade smokers can be made to accommodate more than many commercial smokers—unless you go for a really professional piece of equipment. If you are making your own, make sure you have plenty of rods, hooks, and racks, so that you can really make the most of the space. Fish and sausages can be hung, either threaded through skewers, hooked onto butcher's hooks, or threaded with string to hang them up.

WHICH WOOD TO USE

There are no fixed rules when it comes to pairing woods with meat and fish. I've suggested some woods for smoking below but as you gain in experience you will get to know your own preferences.

What is really important, however, is to use a pure, natural hardwood that is untreated and organic if possible. Do use your own cuttings and sawdust if you have trees. Wood chunks or chips can be used in large hot smokers, small chips in stovetop smokers, and sawdust is used in portable smokers. Place a plastic sheet underneath the tree as it's being cut to gather the sawdust. If you are using a saw, oil it with vegetable or sunflower oil. Do not use a chainsaw that is oiled with a chain oil, as this is toxic and will contaminate the smoke. Softwoods, such as pine and fir, must be avoided.

WHAT OTHER MATERIALS CAN YOU USE TO SMOKE?

To create a more aromatic smoke, try using hay, bay leaves, lavender, juniper branches, nettles, pine needles (not pine wood, though, which can contain toxic resins), and rosemary sprigs, toward the end of your smoking time. Feel free to experiment with the combinations of smoking material you use.

TO SOAK OR NOT TO SOAK?

Soaking your chips, chunks, or dust in water will encourage them to smolder, rather than burn. But you can absolutely put the chips on dry—it is up to you. Why not try both approaches and see which you prefer? I often don't soak mine when I'm in a hurry. The wood can be soaked for as little as an hour—or as long as you like—and drained well before being placed on top of the charcoal.

WHAT ABOUT CHARCOAL?

As with your wood, the charcoal needs to be completely natural. I use a 100 percent organic charcoal that is a mix of oak and hickory. Try visiting your local butcher or hardware store—you may well find a local charcoal for sale. This is a growing market, and there are a huge number of small artisanal producers in operation. Just make sure you don't use briquettes or

HARDWOOD TYPE	INGREDIENT
Alder	Poultry and fish
Apple	Poultry, fish, cheese, ham, and game
Ash	Pork, fish, poultry, and lamb
Beech	Pork, fish, poultry, lamb, and cheese
Birch	Pork and poultry
Cherry	Duck and game, especially venison
Chestnut	Cheese
Hickory	Beef and pork
Maple	Cheese, pork, poultry, and vegetables
Mesquite	Beef, pork, lamb, and vegetables
Oak	Beef, pork, and game
Pear	Cheese and poultry

lump charcoal that has been treated in any way, as the chemicals involved will be transferred to the ingredients during the smoking process.

HOW TO LIGHT YOUR FIRE?

Light the fire with charcoal, either in your hot or cold smoker incinerator. Fill generously with charcoal, following instructions if you are using a grill, and sprinkle over a couple of handfuls of chips before lighting with a natural firelighter. Do not use any lighters that contain lighter fuel. This process is followed for large hot smokers and cold smokers, when lighting the incinerator chamber. Stovetop hot smokers are lit using dry, small chips, which are placed in the center of the base of the smoker and lit, and sawdust in portable smokers is lit with denatured alcohol.

WHERE TO SMOKE?

Stovetop smokers are the only smokers that can be used indoors. Contrary to expectations, they don't produce too much smoke in the house, as the smoking process takes place with the lid closed and the smoke contained. It is sensible, though, to ensure that the kitchen door is closed at all times, the exhaust fan is on throughout the process, and a window or door is open. This just helps to avoid smells developing and lingering in the house, and setting off sensitive smoke alarms.

All other hot and cold smokers must be used outdoors. You don't need much space to do this, but do make sure you are working away

from plants, small children, animals, and anything flammable.

Obviously, the great outdoors is ideal for smoking, but the need to take sensible precautions still applies, and do bear in mind you will have hot equipment and possibly hot coals to deal with unless you wait for a couple of hours for everything to cool down after you have finished.

Above: The Big Green Egg hot smoker set with charcoal and wood chips. The firelighters have just been lit and the fire is starting to take.

FISH

COLD-SMOKED SIDE OF SALMON

Smoked salmon—which is cold-smoked salmon—is one of the most recognizable smoked ingredients across the world. Properly smoked salmon is a real treat, and the good news is that it is quite simple and sometimes cheaper to make yourself. Home-smoked salmon makes a very special gift if you can't manage a whole piece.

It is important to use a great quality piece of salmon, one that is very, very fresh. If you can't be certain the salmon is sparklingly fresh, then hot smoke (page 23), bake it, or poach it. Freshness is imperative when it comes to cold smoking.

Salmon needs to be filleted before smoking, and do make sure any pin bones are removed. But don't forget you can cold smoke one or two fillets simultaneously. It really doesn't take much of your time to prepare—just your presence.

MAKES 1 SIDE OF SMOKED SALMON

3 quarts water
2½ cups salt
1 side of very fresh salmon, skin on

Start by brining the salmon. Mix the water and salt together in a large Pyrex, glass, or ceramic roasting dish or bowl. Lay the salmon fillet flat in the dish and let brine in the fridge for 3 hours.

Remove from the brine and pat dry. Next, you need to ensure the salmon is really dry. The best way to do this is to return it to the fridge for 12 to 24 hours before smoking.

Hang the salmon in the cold smoker and then light it. Leave the salmon to cold smoke for 12 to 24 hours, depending on how strong you would like the smoky flavor to be; I am usually quite happy to leave it for 12 hours but it can be left for up to 36 hours, if you like a really smoky flavor. The salmon will become a gorgeous coral color and will look slightly translucent. Return the salmon to the fridge and leave for another 12 to 24 hours before slicing and eating.

This salmon will keep, well wrapped, for a week in the fridge. I like to slice it as I go, rather than slice it all once. It can be frozen for up to 3 months, but it is best eaten fresh.

COLD-SMOKED SALMON PLATTER WITH WHOLE-WHEAT BREAD, MUSTARD AND DILL SAUCE, AND PICKLES

This platter makes a stunning lunch or appetizer. It is really nice to serve to guests when entertaining as it is easy to make and can be prepared in advance.

Simply arrange the salmon and bread on a platter, and serve with the mustard and dill sauce and pickles in separate bowls.

SERVES 6

2 to 3 slices cold-smoked salmon per person (page 16)
1 loaf whole-wheat or soda bread, sliced (see below)
Mustard and Dill Sauce (page 20)
Pickled Cucumber (page 20)

WHOLE-WHEAT BREAD

This is a wonderfully useful recipe. Whole-wheat bread is slightly sweet with a tender, dense crust. It is best eaten very fresh, just sliced and buttered, but it toasts well on the second day, if you do have any left over.

Preheat the oven to 375°F. Grease a 9 x 5-inch loaf pan with neutral vegetable oil and set aside.

Start by pouring the milk into a glass measuring cup. Add the lemon juice to the milk and stir. Set aside until required. The lemon juice will sour the milk and turn it into homemade buttermilk.

Sift the flours, salt, and baking soda into a large mixing bowl. Stir to combine. Add the oats, reserving 2 tablespoons to sprinkle on top of the loaf. Stir again.

Now, whisk the honey and molasses into the soured milk. Pour the wet mixture into the dry ingredients in the mixing bowl and stir gently to just combine. Gently spoon the bread mixture into your prepared loaf pan. Smooth off the top of the loaf and sprinkle with the reserved oats.

Bake for 45 to 55 minutes until browned and the crust is crisp. Let cool in the pan for 10 minutes before transferring to a wire rack to cool.

Serve warm, fresh out the oven or when just cool. It must be eaten very fresh. It freezes superbly and keeps for up to 3 days.

vegetable oil, for greasing
2 cups whole milk
2 tablespoons fresh lemon juice
2 cups all-purpose flour
2 cups whole-wheat flour
1 teaspoon sea salt
2 teaspoons baking soda
2 cups rolled oats
1½ tablespoons honey
1½ tablespoons blackstrap molasses

MUSTARD AND DILL SAUCE

This is a delicious, light, mayonnaise-style dressing, with the unmistakable flavors of Scandinavia, which pair so well with smoked fish.

1 heaping tablespoon Dijon mustard
1 teaspoon sugar
1 tablespoon white wine vinegar
1 large egg yolk
⅔ cup sunflower oil
1 tablespoon chopped dill fronds
salt and freshly ground black pepper

Put the mustard, sugar, vinegar, and egg yolk in a bowl and whisk gently to combine. Continue to whisk while slowly drizzling the sunflower oil into the bowl. The sauce will thicken quickly. It will take a couple of minutes to emulsify. Do not rush this stage, otherwise the sauce will split. Stir in the dill fronds and season with salt and pepper. Taste and adjust the seasoning if required. Serve chilled. This sauce will keep covered for a week in the fridge.

PICKLED CUCUMBER

A classic sweet pickled cucumber. It is fantastic with salmon, and a wide range of cold meats and cheeses.

MAKES ABOUT 15 SERVINGS

1 large cucumber, unpeeled, finely sliced on a mandolin
1 to 2 large shallots, finely sliced on a mandolin
1 cup granulated sugar
1 teaspoon sea salt
½ cup white wine vinegar

Combine all the ingredients in a bowl. Stir well, to encourage the sugar to dissolve. This is ready to eat immediately, and can be kept covered in the fridge for a month. It will lose some of its vibrant green color, but is perfectly fine to eat.

SMOKED SALMON RILLETTES

This is one of the easiest and most useful smoked salmon recipes to have in your repertoire. It requires just minutes to prepare and a container of rillettes is a great treat to keep in the fridge.

Spread generously on hot, thin toast, rillettes makes a sensational canapé to serve with drinks, or serve with a nicely dressed green salad for an easy lunch.

I like to make this with hot-smoked salmon, but do try this using half hot-smoked and half cold-smoked salmon for a different flavor and texture.

SERVES 10

11 ounces hot-smoked salmon (see opposite)
  or 5½ ounces hot-smoked salmon and
  5½ ounces cold-smoked salmon (page 20)
10 tablespoons salted butter, melted
juice of ½ lemon
sea salt and freshly ground black pepper
freshly grated nutmeg
1 to 2 teaspoons finely chopped fresh herbs,
  such as chervil or dill (optional)
hot toast or Melba toast, to serve

TIP:

To preserve the rillettes for up to 2 weeks, melt an additional 5 tablespoons salted butter and pour the warm, melted butter over the top of the rillettes once the mixture has been transferred to the bowl to chill. This will set on top and form a protective layer, which will seal in the freshness and prevent the salmon from discoloring.

Put the salmon in a mixing bowl. Remove any skin or bones. Using two forks, gently flake the hot-smoked salmon, breaking it up into small flakes. Try to avoid mashing it, though, which will change the texture. Tear or snip the cold-smoked salmon, if using, into small pieces.

Pour the melted butter and lemon juice over the fish, season to taste with salt, pepper, and nutmeg, and stir together until just combined. Taste, check the seasoning, and stir through any herbs if using. The rillettes are very nice without, so this is up to you.

Transfer the rillettes mixture into a bowl, cover with plastic wrap, and refrigerate for at least 4 hours until firm.

Spread on hot toast or Melba toasts to serve. The rillettes will keep for 3 to 5 days, covered, in the fridge.

HOT-SMOKED SALMON

This is an excellent starting point for a journey into hot smoking. Hot smoking salmon is quick and simple to do and produces wonderfully delicious results, especially if you smoke it over oak. A whole side of salmon or fillets work well here—it's up to you. Fillets will have a smokier flavor compared to a side, due to the greater surface area exposed to smoke. Smoke the fish with the skin on to hold it together and remove the skin before adding the salmon to a recipe. If serving fillets whole, the skin can be left on.

Make as much or as little of the rub as you like—just multiply or divide the quantity of salt and sugar in proportion to the amount of salmon you are using.

Mix the salt with the sugar and rub it into the salmon. Place it on a plate or pan and cover with plastic wrap. Refrigerate for at least 30 minutes. Remove the fish from the fridge and rinse under cold running water, then dry using paper towels. Cover the salmon and return the salmon to the fridge for at least 4 hours or overnight if possible.

When you are ready to smoke, set up your hot smoker with oak shavings or chips. For fillets, I like to use a stovetop smoker, and for a side I use a large outdoor smoker. When the smoker is between 140 and 220°F and smoke has appeared, smoke the fish for 20 to 30 minutes until it is golden and no longer looks raw.

Remove from the smoker and either enjoy warm or let cool. If you prefer a more delicate flavor, smoke for 10 to 15 minutes and finish cooking the salmon in the oven, wrapped in foil. Bake fillets for 10 minutes and a side for 20 minutes at 350°F.

The hot-smoked salmon will keep, covered, for up to 3 days in the fridge. It is wonderful served flaked into salads or onto pasta or used in fishcakes and fish pies.

MAKES ABOUT **8** SERVINGS

¼ cup sea salt
¼ cup light brown sugar
1 small side of fresh salmon or 8 fillets of salmon, skin on, weighing about 5½ ounces each

2 tablespoons oak shavings or chips

ASIAN-SPICED HOT-SMOKED SALMON

A stovetop smoker is the ideal piece of equipment to use for hot smoking fillets of fish quickly and easily. This is a gorgeous salmon recipe and I like to serve the whole fillets hot on top of a mix of stir-fried vegetables.

Start by making the marinade for the salmon. Put the soy, honey, sugar, garlic, ginger, and five-spice into a saucepan and stir together. Gently warm it over medium heat for about 5 minutes. Set aside and let cool.

When the marinade is cool, pour it into a shallow dish and add the salmon. Cover with plastic wrap and refrigerate for at least 3 hours or overnight if possible.

Remove the fish from the fridge, lift the fillets out of the marinade, and dry them using paper towels. Discard the marinade, cover the fillets, and return to the fridge for at least 4 hours or overnight if possible.

When you are ready to smoke, set up your hot smoker with oak shavings. When the smoker is between 140 and 220°F and smoke has appeared, smoke the fish for 20 to 30 minutes until it is golden and no longer looks raw.

Once smoked, the salmon will be darker in color and cooked all the way through, or just slightly pink in the thickest part of the fillet. It will keep for up to 3 days in the fridge and can be eaten hot or cold.

SERVES 6

6 salmon fillets, skin on, weighing about 5½ ounces each

FOR THE MARINADE
⅔ cup tamari soy sauce
⅔ cup honey
⅓ cup light brown sugar
2 garlic cloves, crushed
1 tablespoon peeled and finely grated fresh ginger
large pinch of Chinese five-spice powder

2 tablespoons oak shavings or chips

HOT-SMOKED SHRIMP

Shrimp hot smoke very quickly and easily. You can leave the shells on or peel them—it is up to you—but I find small shrimp can benefit from a protective jacket—they can shrink and dry out easily if peeled first and then smoked, and the flavor of the smoke is imparted more intensely. Larger shrimp are more robust and will hold up better to smoking when peeled.

Smoked shrimp are delicious in all types of salads, pies, sandwiches, and pasta dishes.

Serves 4

1¼ pounds fresh shrimp, peeled or unpeeled
2 tablespoons sea salt

The first step is to salt the shrimp. Put them in a shallow pan. Sprinkle with the salt and rub it all over each shrimp. Cover with plastic wrap and transfer to the fridge for 2 hours.

After 2 hours, carefully rinse the salt from each shrimp, drying them very well. When you are ready to smoke, set up your hot smoker with wood shavings or chips. When the smoker is between 140 and 220°F and smoke has appeared, hot smoke the shrimp for 15 to 30 minutes until they turn a coral color tinged with ocher around the edges.

Remove the shrimp from the smoker and let rest in the fridge for at least 30 minutes before using. These shrimp can be stored in the fridge for 3 to 5 days, well wrapped.

SMOKED SHRIMP, PEACH, AND MINT SALAD

Smoked shrimp go so well with peaches and fresh mint leaves. This is such a light, fresh, and vibrant combination of flavors that is very appealing on a hot day. The juicy, chargrilled peaches are the perfect partner to sweet, smoky shrimp. Grill the peaches until warm on a grill pan on the stove or outdoor grill. Handle with care as they will be very soft when ripe.

1 ripe peach, halved, pitted, and cut into ½-inch thick slices
5 tablespoons extra virgin olive oil
1 teaspoon honey
1 teaspoon lemon juice
salt and freshly ground black pepper
7 ounces hot-smoked shrimp (page 26)
10 large mint leaves, thinly sliced
¾ cup pea shoots

Heat a ridged grill pan until it starts to smoke. Place the peach slices carefully onto the grill pan and cook for 1 to 2 minutes on each side until grill lines form. If you are using a barbecue grill, simply cook the peach slices on the grill rack once it is hot. They may only take a minute on a hot barbecue. The peaches will smell fragrant and fruity as they cook. Turn them over and cook for another minute or two on the other side, and then carefully remove the slices and set aside on a plate to cool.

Meanwhile, whisk together the olive oil, honey, and lemon juice in a large mixing bowl, adding salt and pepper to taste. Add the peaches, shrimp, mint, and pea shoots and then gently toss to combine all the ingredients evenly. Serve immediately.

SKAGENRÖRA

I've spent a lot of time in Scandinavia, and adore so many smoked fish recipes typical of the region. Incredibly good open sandwiches made with *Skagenröra*—creamy smoked shrimp salad—are widely enjoyed for lunch in Sweden.

To make these sandwiches even more delicious, it is really worth keeping your eyes peeled for a great, fresh rye bread, if you can get ahold of one from an artisan baker. It will taste infinitely superior to supermarket rye breads, which can be very dry.

You may not require four sandwiches at once—if not, store the filling covered in the fridge for up to 3 days and make up just one or two sandwiches at a time.

There is very little work involved here. Start by mixing the crème fraîche and mayonnaise together in a small mixing bowl. Add the shrimp, lemon juice, and season with salt and pepper, adding Tabasco sauce to taste. Taste and make sure you are happy with the flavor of the dressing.

To serve, place the rye bread on a plate. Top each slice with a large lettuce leaf and spoon the shrimp in dressing over the lettuce. Serve immediately, scattered with fresh dill, if you'd like.

SERVES 4

⅓ cup full-fat crème fraîche
⅓ cup best-quality mayonnaise—homemade is nicest
2 pounds hot-smoked, peeled shrimp (page 26)
juice of ½ lemon, plus lemon wedges, to serve
sea salt and freshly ground black pepper
a few drops Tabasco sauce
4 large slices very fresh rye bread
4 large lettuce leaves—a simple butter leaf or iceberg lettuce is ideal
2 teaspoons chopped fresh dill fronds (optional)

HOT-SMOKED MACKEREL

Mackerel is possibly the cheapest and easiest fish to smoke. Try it in salads, sandwiches, pasta, croquettes, tarts, or fishcakes.

Mackerel can be hot-smoked whole or in fillets. Whole mackerel will need smoking for a longer time than fillets, for a full smoky flavor.

SERVES 4

4 fresh mackerel, filleted, skin on
1 tablespoon sea salt

2 tablespoons oak shavings or chips

Simply sprinkle the mackerel with sea salt and leave, covered in the fridge, for 2 hours. Rinse and dry well. When you are ready to smoke, set up your hot smoker with wood shavings or chips. When the smoker is between 140 and 220°F and smoke has appeared, smoke the fish for 15 to 45 minutes until the flesh is cooked through and lightly golden. Oak is a nice wood to use here.

Wrap the mackerel once smoked and cooled and store in the fridge for 12 to 24 hours before eating. It will keep for 3 to 5 days in the fridge, well wrapped.

HOT-SMOKED HADDOCK

Smoked haddock is a wonderfully useful ingredient. Flake it into rich, cheesy omelets, fishcakes, or fish pies, or serve it with buttered spinach and a poached egg for breakfast. Properly smoked haddock takes on a wonderful golden hue that is so much more attractive than the traditional yellow-dyed smoked fillets.

Haddock can be hot or cold smoked, but hot-smoked haddock is a much more versatile ingredient. For cold-smoked haddock, treat a whole haddock fillet in the same way as the cold-smoked salmon recipe on page 16. Cold-smoked haddock is delicious served thinly sliced, just like cold-smoked salmon.

SERVES 2 AS A MAIN AND 4 AS AN APPETIZER

1 large fresh haddock fillet, weighing about
    10½ to 14 ounces, skin on and pin bones
    removed
¼ cup sea salt

Place the haddock in a shallow pan. Sprinkle with the salt and rub into the surface. Cover the fish with plastic wrap and transfer to the fridge for 2 hours.

After 2 hours, rinse the salt from the fish and dry the fillet well. When you are ready to smoke, set up your hot smoker with wood shavings or chips. When the smoker is between 140 and 220°F and smoke has appeared, smoke the fish for 30 minutes to 1 hour until the fillet is lightly golden around the edges.

Remove from the smoker and let rest for at least 30 minutes before using. It will keep in the fridge for 3 to 5 days, well wrapped.

ASIAN SMOKED MACKEREL SALAD

This salad is amazingly vibrant, packed full of interesting flavors and textures.

Add the oil to a large nonstick frying pan. Turn the heat to high and add the mackerel. Fry for just a minute or two until crispy. Remove from the heat and lay the mackerel fillets on paper towels to absorb any excess oil.

Put the prepared mango, carrot, shallot, and chile in a large mixing bowl. Stir together. Stir the sugar, fish sauce, lime zest, and juice together in a small bowl. Pour over the salad ingredients in the bowl. Add the mackerel and gently combine. Serve on a plate topped with peanuts and Thai basil, if you're using it. Enjoy immediately.

SERVES 2 AS A MAIN COURSE

1 teaspoon sunflower oil
4 small hot-smoked mackerel fillets, skin
  removed (page 32)
1 mango, peeled and cut into ½-inch dice
1 large carrot, peeled and grated or cut into
  fine julienne
½ small shallot, peeled and very thinly sliced
1 red chile, seeded and thinly sliced
2 teaspoons granulated or palm sugar
4 teaspoons Thai fish sauce
zest and juice of 2 limes
¼ cup roasted salted peanuts, coarsely
  chopped
½ cup Thai basil, thinly sliced or left whole
  (optional)

SMOKED HADDOCK MOUSSE WITH LEMON HOLLANDAISE AND SHRIMP

This mousse makes a fantastically delicious and impressive appetizer. It is surprisingly straightforward to make, and much of the preparation can be done in advance. For this recipe you need 4-inch ramekins. Pillivuyt makes my favorite ramekins—their Size 1 is ideal here.

SERVES 6

butter, for greasing

FOR THE MOUSSE

10½ ounces hot-smoked haddock fillet (page 32), skin and bones removed, chopped into small pieces
2 extra large eggs, beaten
1 cup heavy cream
sea salt, freshly ground black pepper, and freshly grated nutmeg

FOR THE LEMON HOLLANDAISE AND SHRIMP

4 large egg yolks
4 teaspoons fresh lemon juice
10 tablespoons salted butter, melted
8 ounces cooked shrimp, peeled

Before you get cooking, butter 6 x 4-inch ramekins well and set aside.

To make the mousse, put the fish, eggs, cream, salt, pepper, and nutmeg into a food processor and blend until smooth. Divide the mixture evenly between the ramekins, cover with plastic wrap, and chill for 3 hours. You can chill them for longer if you are preparing the mousse to serve later in the day.

Next, prepare the hollandaise. This can be made in advance and kept warm in a thermos. I like to prepare this about an hour before serving, so it's really fresh. Set a large heatproof bowl over a pan of hot water and place over a low heat on the stove. Add the egg yolks, lemon juice, and 2 teaspoons of cold water and whisk together. Gradually, pour in the melted butter, whisking continuously, until the hollandaise is thick. Season to taste with salt, pepper, and nutmeg. Add the shrimp, stirring them in very gently. Taste again. Pour into the thermos immediately. Seal the lid and set aside. The hollandaise is now ready to pour onto the freshly cooked mousse.

When you are ready to cook the mousse, preheat the oven to 375°F. Stand the ramekins in a large, high-sided roasting pan and pour in enough boiling water so that it comes halfway up the sides of the ramekins. Bake for 30 minutes.

Remove the ramekins from the oven and stand for 2 to 3 minutes before turning out onto hot plates. Serve immediately with the hollandaise poured over the top.

SMOKED HADDOCK AND
SHRIMP FISH PIE

This is a luxurious, smoky, creamy fish pie, with an herby white wine sauce and plenty of cheesy potatoes on top. It's my favorite fish pie recipe because the sauce has so much flavor and the cheesy mashed potato topping is just irresistible—I hope it will become yours, too.

1¼ pounds hot-smoked haddock fillet (page 32)
1¼ pounds raw shrimp, peeled
1 organic lemon, halved
¾ cup dry white wine
½ cup chicken or fish stock
green salad or green vegetables, to serve

For the sauce
4 tablespoons salted butter
½ cup all-purpose flour
1 cup heavy cream
1 bunch of fresh dill fronds, finely chopped
1 bunch of fresh flat-leaf parsley, finely chopped
sea salt and freshly ground black pepper

For the potato topping
1¾ pounds potatoes, peeled and cut into large chunks
5 tablespoons salted butter
¼ to ½ cup heavy cream (depending on the variety of potato)
¾ cup Cheddar, grated

Put the fish, shrimp, lemon halves, and wine in a pan. Add sufficient cold water to cover and poach the fish for 5 minutes. Remove the fish and shrimp from the water using a spatula, leaving the liquid in the pan. Discard the lemon.

To make the sauce, boil the poaching liquid in the pan until reduced in volume to ½ cup, and then add the stock.

Melt the butter in a separate pan then add the flour and cook for 2 to 3 minutes, stirring continuously. Add the stock mixture a little at a time, whisking thoroughly until it's all incorporated and the sauce is smooth. Remove from the heat and stir in the cream, dill, and parsley. Season to taste and set aside.

For the mashed potato topping, boil the potatoes in salted water until cooked, drain, and mash with the butter, cream, and cheese. Season to taste. Place the fish and shrimp in an 8 x 12 x 2-inch ovenproof dish, pour over the sauce, and top with the potato. You can either pipe this on, or spoon it, evenly coating the top and smoothing it out using a spatula or ruffling it up using a fork. The pie is ready to be baked or it can be kept in the fridge, covered, to bake later in the day.

Bake the fish pie in a preheated oven at 350°F for 25 to 35 minutes until piping hot. The mashed potato topping should be a rich brown color and the creamy sauce should be bubbling around the edges.

Serve with a green salad or green vegetables.

SCANDINAVIAN FISKEFRIKADELLER

These smoked haddock fishcakes are inspired by my travels in Denmark, where fishcakes are extremely popular, and are made with a very high fish content.

Put all the ingredients for the fishcakes in a food processor and pulse until you have a smooth mixture. Chill the mixture, covered, in the fridge for 2 to 4 hours until firm.

Form the mixture into 8 fishcakes and coat each one lightly in flour. Heat the butter and oil in a large nonstick frying pan and fry the fishcakes for 3 to 4 minutes until golden on both sides and cooked through.

Serve with Celeriac and caper remoulade and Fennel salad (below).

SERVES 4 GENEROUSLY

1¼ pounds hot-smoked haddock (page 32), skin and bones removed and cut into large chunks
1 teaspoon sea salt
2 large eggs, beaten
3 tablespoons all-purpose flour, plus extra for coating
1 large potato, peeled, chopped, boiled, and drained
½ bunch of fresh dill fronds, finely chopped
freshly ground black pepper

FOR FRYING
2 teaspoons salted butter
2 tablespoons sunflower or vegetable oil

CELERIAC AND CAPER REMOULADE

This is a great winter salad that also goes very well with cold meats and even with the hot dogs on page 100.

Whisk together the mayonnaise, lemon juice, and mustard in a large bowl. Stir in the grated celeriac and the capers. Season to taste with salt and freshly ground pepper. Keep the remoulade chilled in the fridge until you are ready to serve. It will keep for up to 3 days in the fridge.

SERVES 4 TO 6

¾ cup best-quality mayonnaise—homemade is nicest
juice of ½ lemon
3 teaspoons Dijon mustard
1 pound celeriac, peeled and finely grated
3 heaping teaspoons capers, drained and rinsed
sea salt and freshly ground black pepper

FENNEL SALAD

Fennel pairs very well with the smokiness of the fishcakes. This is a very light, fresh, and crunchy salad that is delicious with all kinds of grilled or broiled fish.

Simply place all the ingredients in a large mixing bowl, mix together, and serve. The fennel salad will keep, covered, for up to 2 days, in the fridge.

SERVES 4

1 fennel bulb, thinly sliced on a mandolin
1 tablespoon olive oil
1 teaspoon sugar
1 tablespoon good-quality cider vinegar
½ bunch of fresh dill fronds, chopped

HERRING AND KIPPERS

Not everyone knows this but kippers are, in fact, smoked herring. The fish are gutted and split open down the back and smoked quite heavily, using a blend of woods, often including oak.

Kippers can be traced back at least to the 1300s in the British Isles, probably made as a way of preserving an abundance of fresh fish. Groups of fishermen and "herring girls" skilled in filleting the catch lived a nomadic existence following shoals down the east coast of England, catching and filleting the fresh herring, which was traditionally caught between mid-May and late September. Herring are no longer so abundant but if you happen to be in Northumberland, do visit one of the traditional smokehouses on the coast—it's a real experience.

Kippers were the quintessential Victorian and Edwardian breakfast, and are enjoying a comeback of late, thanks to their low cost and high nutritional value.

There are conflicting opinions on how best to cook kippers—either placed in a bowl of boiling water to warm through—which is very quick and easy—or grilled, which retains the oils in the flesh.

I have two options for you here. First, is a light hot-smoked herring, which is wonderful used in salads—do try the Scandinavian-inspired herring salad on page 45. Second, is the more traditional kipper. While it is possible to buy excellent kippers at a reasonable price, it is really fun to try making your own.

HOT-SMOKED HERRING FILLETS

Serves 4

4 fresh herring, gutted, cleaned, and filleted
1 tablespoon sea salt

2 tablespoons oak shavings or chips

Sprinkle the herring fillets with sea salt and leave, covered in the fridge, for 2 hours. Rinse and dry well. When you are ready to smoke, set up your hot smoker with wood shavings or chips. When the smoker is between 140 and 220°F and smoke has appeared, smoke the fish for 15 to 45 minutes until the flesh is cooked through and lightly golden in color. Oak is a nice wood to use here.

Serve warm or cold with salads, eggs, or on hot, buttered toast.

TRADITIONAL KIPPERS

It is easier than you think to make a classic kipper at home.

Start by preparing the herring. Split the whole fish down the back, running your knife along the length of the belly to open the fish out.

Next, brine the fish. Mix the water and salt together in a large roasting dish or bowl. Add the herring and set aside to brine for 3 hours in the fridge.

Remove the fish from the brine and dry them well with paper towels. Light the cold smoker (see page 11). Hook the herrings by the head using a butcher's hook, and hang them inside the smoker, ensuring they are well spaced, and leave to cold smoke for 12 to 16 hours, depending on how strong you would like the smoky flavor to taste. The kippers can be left for longer—up to 24 hours, if you like a really smoky flavor. The kippers take on a gorgeous golden color, but won't be as dark as some commercial kippers. Keep them for up to a week in the fridge, wrapped in wax paper.

SERVES 4 PEOPLE

4 very fresh herring, gutted and cleaned
3 quarts water
2½ cups salt

HERRING, POTATO, AND WATERCRESS SALAD

This is a hearty salad that makes an excellent lunch or substantial appetizer. It is inspired by the flavors of Scandinavia.

Start by making the dressing. Put all the ingredients into a glass measuring cup and whisk together. Taste and adjust the seasoning if necessary.

Boil the potatoes until tender. Drain and, when cooled just enough to handle, halve and toss in the dressing. Let cool.

Carefully flake the herring into pieces and mix gently with the potatoes, shallot, and dill. Add the watercress, toss through gently, and season. Divide the watercress between four plates and spoon the potatoes and herring on top.

SERVES 4

FOR THE DRESSING
½ tablespoon whole-grain mustard
½ teaspoon Dijon mustard
1 tablespoon cider vinegar
3 tablespoons olive oil
¼ teaspoon sugar
sea salt and freshly ground black pepper

FOR THE HERRING
14 ounces small new potatoes
10½ ounces hot-smoked herring fillets (page 42)
1 small shallot, halved and very thinly sliced
1 tablespoon chopped fresh dill fronds
large handful of watercress

KIPPERS FLORENTINE

This is a really special breakfast and a delicious and quick way to enjoy the full smoky flavor of kippers.

2 kippers (page 45)
1 tablespoon salted butter
7 ounces spinach
2 extra large, very fresh eggs
salt and freshly ground black pepper

Put the kippers in a bowl and cover with boiling water. Set aside and leave for 10 minutes to warm.

Melt the butter in a large nonstick frying pan or wok. Add the spinach, then stir gently with a spatula or tongs to encourage it to wilt. Once collapsed, set aside.

Meanwhile, poach the eggs by cracking them into boiling water. Reduce the heat so they sit in the water for 3 to 4 minutes until the white is firm, but the yolk is still runny. You may need to spoon hot water over the top of the eggs to ensure the tops are set. Carefully lift the eggs out of the water using a slotted spoon and sit on some paper towels on a plate to absorb any excess water.

Drain the kippers and prepare as fillets, by carefully removing the fillets from the bone, if required. Serve the spinach on a plate, topped with the kippers and eggs. Season and serve immediately.

SMOKED TROUT

Trout is a delicious, versatile freshwater fish that makes an excellent and cheaper alternative to salmon. Like salmon, it can either be hot- or cold-smoked.

HOT-SMOKED TROUT

This is a quick way to smoke trout and is really delicious flaked and added to salads, fishcakes, or stirred through pasta. A stovetop smoker is a very useful and quick way of smoking trout fillets.

Makes 4 fillets

2 trout, filleted, skin on
1 tablespoon sea salt

Place the trout fillets in a shallow dish or bowl, sprinkle with the salt, and rub it into the surface. Cover the fish with plastic wrap and leave it for 2 hours in the fridge.

After 2 hours, rinse the salt from the fish and dry the fillets well with paper towels. When you are ready to smoke, set up your hot smoker with wood shavings or chips. When the smoker is between 140 and 220°F and smoke has appeared, smoke the fish for 20 to 30 minutes until the fillets are cooked and lightly golden around the edges.

Remove from the smoker and let rest for at least 30 minutes before using. Hot-smoked trout can be stored in the fridge, well wrapped, for up to 5 days.

COLD-SMOKED TROUT

Cold-smoked trout makes a delicious, and more economical, alternative to traditional cold-smoked salmon.

Start by brining the trout. Mix the water and salt together in a large Pyrex, glass, or ceramic dish or bowl. Add the fish and leave to brine for 2 hours in the fridge.

Remove the trout fillets from the brine and pat dry with paper towels. Light the cold smoker (see page 11). Hook the fillets with a butcher's hook and hang, well-spaced out, to cold smoke for 12 to 24 hours, depending on how strong you prefer the smoky flavor to be. The trout will have a lovely coral color and will look slightly translucent. Leave the trout (don't be tempted to eat it yet!) in the fridge for another 12 hours before slicing and eating.

Cold-smoked trout keeps for up to 1 week in the fridge, well wrapped. I like to slice it as I go, rather than slice it all at once.

MAKES 4 FILLETS

3 quarts water
2½ cups salt
2 trout, filleted, skin on

2 tablespoons apple wood shavings or chips

FRESH TAGLIATELLE WITH
SMOKED TROUT AND WATERCRESS

This is a wonderful everyday recipe for a super-quick but delicious supper. This recipe is very relaxed, so feel free to adjust the quantities as you like. Hot- or cold-smoked trout both work very nicely here.

1 pound fresh tagliatelle
¾ cup full-fat crème fraîche
7 ounces hot- or cold-smoked trout (pages 48 to 49), flaked or cut into small strips
juice of ½ to 1 lemon, to taste
sea salt and freshly ground black pepper
2 cups fresh watercress leaves, coarsely chopped
2 tablespoons chopped fresh flat-leaf parsley, dill, or chives
¼ cup Parmesan, grated
green salad, to serve (optional)

Bring a very large pan of salted water to a boil to cook the tagliatelle.

While it is coming to a boil, make the sauce for the pasta. Put the crème fraîche in a small pan and gently warm for a couple of minutes. Add the trout and lemon juice, to taste, and stir through. Season generously. Continue to warm it for another minute or two.

Meanwhile, cook the tagliatelle according to the package instructions. Once it is cooked, drain well. Set in a colander over the pan for a minute to drain fully while you finish off the sauce.

Add the watercress and herbs to the pan, taste and adjust the seasoning if needed, and stir well to combine all the ingredients. Plenty of black pepper is nice here.

Stir the pasta sauce through the tagliatelle—I find it is easiest to do this in the pan the pasta was cooked in—pouring out any water before transferring the pasta back into this pan and adding the sauce on top.

Serve the pasta in warmed bowls, topped with Parmesan. A green salad works very nicely on the side, too, accompanied by a chilled glass of white.

HOT-SMOKED TROUT PÂTÉ WITH SOURDOUGH TOASTS

This pâté is both delicious and impressive and yet it takes just minutes to put together—ideal to serve with drinks, as a light appetizer, or for lunch. Using hot-smoked trout provides a warm, well-rounded flavor, and a gorgeous creamy texture.

Put the trout in a mixing bowl. Use your hands to gently flake the flesh. Add the sour cream, capers, and sea salt and stir carefully to combine. Finally, stir in the herbs, if using. For a chunky finish, stir very gently, or for a smoother finish, break the fish flakes up as you mix the ingredients together. That's all there is to do. Serve the pâté chilled in a bowl.

Toast the sourdough slices at the last minute, and serve them warm. They will crisp up very quickly as they cool. Enjoy the pâté as soon as the toasts are ready.

SERVES 2 AS A MAIN OR 4 AS AN APPETIZER

2 hot-smoked trout fillets (page 48), skin removed
⅓ cup full-fat sour cream
1 tablespoon nonpareil capers, drained
generous pinch of sea salt flakes
1 teaspoon chopped fresh dill fronds or flat-leaf parsley (optional)
4 to 6 x ⅛-inch thick slices of sourdough bread, halved

HOT-SMOKED MONKFISH

Hot smoking adds an extra layer of deliciousness to the delicate, sweet flavor of monkfish. Cheeks will smoke just as well as tail, but you may need to adjust your cooking times depending on the thickness of the fillet. Monkfish can be cold-smoked and served raw in the same way as haddock can, but I think it is best, and most versatile, when it is hot smoked.

Start by salting the fish. Place the fillets or cheeks in a shallow dish or bowl. Sprinkle with the salt and rub it into the flesh. Cover with plastic wrap and leave for 2 hours in the fridge.

After 2 hours, rinse the salt from the fish, pat the fillet dry with paper towels, and hot smoke (see page 11) for 30 minutes to 1 hour until the white flesh is lightly golden around the edges.

Remove from the smoker and let rest for at least 30 minutes before using. Hot-smoked monkfish can be stored, well wrapped, in the fridge for up to 5 days.

MAKES 2 LARGE FILLETS OR 4 CHEEKS

¼ cup sea salt
2 large monkfish tail fillets or 4 whole monkfish cheeks

SMOKED MONKFISH WITH PROSCIUTTO AND ROSEMARY

Smoked monkfish has a delicate flavor and it tastes wonderful when it is wrapped in prosciutto and roasted. These parcels make an easy and impressive dinner.

Preheat the oven to 350°F.

Start by seasoning the monkfish fillets with salt and pepper. Place a sprig of rosemary on each piece and wrap each one in prosciutto using 2 slices per portion. Sit the parcels on a nonstick baking sheet and bake for 20 to 25 minutes until the prosciutto is really crispy.

Serve as soon as the fish is cooked, with some wilted buttered spinach and lemon wedges on the side.

SERVES 4

4 generous chunks hot-smoked monkfish, weighing about 5½ ounces each
sea salt and freshly ground black pepper
4 small sprigs of fresh rosemary
8 slices prosciutto
wilted spinach and lemon wedges, to serve

HOT-SMOKED SCALLOPS

Scallops are wonderful served hot or cold. In the Hebrides, fresh, hand-dived scallops are often smoked with peat, which imparts a unique flavor. I recommend buying them by mail order to smoke using wood at home. Scallops are meaty and rich: depending on size, allow 2 to 3 per person.

Place the scallops in a shallow dish or bowl. Sprinkle with the salt and rub it over each scallop. Cover with plastic wrap and transfer to the fridge for 2 hours.

After 2 hours, carefully rinse the salt from each morsel, drying them very well with paper towels. When you are ready to smoke, set up your hot smoker with wood shavings or chips. When the smoker is between 140 and 220°F and smoke has appeared, smoke the scallops for 30 minutes to 1 hour until the flesh is lightly golden at the edges. A stovetop smoker is ideal for this.

Remove the scallops from the smoker and let rest for at least 30 minutes before serving. Hot-smoked scallops can be stored, well wrapped, in the fridge for 3 to 5 days.

MAKES 8

8 fresh scallops
2 tablespoons sea salt

SMOKED SCALLOP SALAD WITH BACON AND PUY LENTILS

Smoked scallops can be enjoyed both hot and cold. Either serve them cold, cut into slices, or pan-fry in a bit of olive oil or bacon fat to crisp them up. They need just 2 minutes on each side to cook them perfectly.

Gently fry the bacon in a pan over medium-high heat until very crisp. You may need to add a teaspoon of oil if the bacon is lean and doesn't render much fat. This should take about 15 minutes.

Meanwhile, make the dressing by mixing all the ingredients together in a large bowl. Season, add the lentils to the dressing, and stir through so they absorb the flavors nicely.

Just before you are ready to serve, add the leaves to the bowl and stir through. Add the bacon, too. If you are serving the scallops warm, pan-fry in the bacon fat for 2 minutes on each side.

Divide the salad onto plates and top with slices of cold scallop or freshly pan-fried warm scallops. Enjoy immediately.

SERVES 4

5½ ounces thick-cut smoked bacon, cut thinly
1 teaspoon olive oil (optional)
1¼ cups cooked Puy lentils
5½ ounces watercress, arugula, or mâche
8 large smoked scallops

FOR THE DRESSING
6 to 8 tablespoons extra virgin olive oil
1½ tablespoons balsamic vinegar
¼ teaspoon Dijon mustard
1 tablespoon fresh lemon juice
2 tablespoons finely chopped fresh flat-leaf parsley
sea salt and freshly ground black pepper

SMOKED COD ROE

I suspect most people have tried cod roe in the form of taramasalata, but not on its own. It is delicious sliced thinly and spread on hot, buttered sourdough toast, perhaps with a squeeze of lemon.

SERVES UP TO 8

¾ cup salt
1 quart cold water
2 fresh whole cod roe

Dissolve the salt in the water in a large Pyrex, glass, or ceramic dish or bowl. Add the cod roe and transfer to the fridge to brine for 2 hours. Lift the roe out of the brine and dry it very well.

Set up your cold smoker (see page 11) and cold smoke for 24 hours. The color of the roe will darken significantly. It will keep wrapped well in the fridge for up to 2 weeks.

TARAMASALATA

To make a delicious, authentic taramasalata—quite different from store-bought—try this simple recipe.

SERVES 4 TO 6

9 ounces smoked cod roe (see above), cut in
  half and the flesh scooped out
2 large slices of sourdough bread
2 tablespoons whole milk
juice of 1 lemon
2 tablespoons sunflower oil
2 tablespoons extra virgin olive oil

Put all the ingredients in a food processor and pulse until smooth. Pour into a bowl, cover, and refrigerate until required. Serve as part of a mezze platter with toasted pita bread and some Kalamata olives.

SMOKED COD'S ROE SKAGEN

Skagen are hugely addictive toasts topped with fish—they are very popular in Scandinavia. This smoked fish spread is not for the faint-hearted. It is intensely smoky and fishy. I like it spread thinly on toasted bread or brioche and topped with a few peeled shrimp. They are heavenly served with a good glass of champagne before a meal or for a light lunch.

Put the roe in a food processor, add the lemon juice, crème fraîche, and oil, and season well. Pulse in the processor to form a smooth-ish spread. Taste, to check the seasoning.

Serve on slices of hot toasted sourdough or brioche, with some lemon wedges on the side.

SERVES **8**

9 ounces smoked cod roe (see opposite), cut in half and the flesh scooped out
juice of 1 large lemon
2 tablespoons full-fat crème fraîche
2 tablespoons extra virgin olive oil
sea salt and freshly ground black pepper
toasted sourdough bread or good-quality brioche, sliced, and lemon wedges, to serve

DAIRY

SMOKED MOZZARELLA

Like salmon or other fish, smoked mozzarella is another wonderfully versatile ingredient to cook with. You may have seen *scamorza*, an Italian smoked mozzarella, on sale. Traditionally made in Apulia and Calabria in southern Italy, it is much firmer than fresh mozzarella as it has been aged as well as smoked. Its shape is rather peculiar as it is tied with string around the middle and hung up to smoke and dry. The Italians call it "strangled" rather than tied! This recipe provides a quick way to smoke fresh mozzarella at home.

MAKES 13 OUNCES

3 x 4½-ounce balls of fresh mozzarella, thoroughly dried

Place the wood chips in the top pan in the cold smoker until about two-thirds full, then add 1 to 3 handfuls of chips on top of that and light it. Chestnut, maple, or pear wood chips all work well. Put the cheese in a small, shallow dish as it can leak a little whey when smoking. When the smoker is at the correct stage (see page 11), add the cheese and smoke for 30 minutes. Store, well wrapped in plastic wrap, in the fridge for up to a week.

SMOKED RICOTTA

Ricotta's flavor is very subtle and smoking it is a fun way to add an extra dimension to a plain but versatile ingredient. The combination of rich creaminess and smoke works well in a wide range of dishes.

MAKES 9 OUNCES

9 ounces fresh ricotta, drained and very well dried

Place the wood chips in the top pan in the cold smoker until about two-thirds full, then add 1 to 3 handfuls of chips on top of that and light it. Chestnut, maple, or pear wood chips all work well. When it is at the correct stage (see page 11), place the ricotta in a small, nonmetallic, heatproof bowl or dish and smoke for 30 minutes. Tightly wrap the smoked ricotta (in its dish) in plastic wrap and store in the fridge for up to a week.

SMOKED CHEDDAR

Gentle cold smoking adds an addictive extra layer of flavor to Cheddar cheese. Try oak or apple wood, which are a particularly good match with Cheddar. Artisanal cheeses work best for smoking, as they are firmer and less fatty than more commercial options.

MAKES 10½ OUNCES

10½ ounces aged, full-flavored Cheddar

Place the wood chips in the top pan in the cold smoker until about two-thirds full, then add 1 to 3 handfuls of chips on top of that and light it. Chestnut, maple, or pear wood chips all work well. When it is at the correct stage (see page 11), add the cheese and smoke for 30 minutes. Wrap the cheese well in plastic wrap and store in the fridge for up to a month.

SMOKED CHEDDAR, MUSHROOM, AND LEEK TART

This is a really delicious, creamy, deep-filled quiche. It makes a special lunch to serve to guests and also travels very well, making excellent outdoor eating. Smoked Cheddar pairs fantastically with the deep, earthy flavor of the mushrooms. Do make sure you use brown mushrooms, rather than white, as they are much more flavorful.

Start by making the pastry dough. Put the flour, butter, and salt in a large mixing bowl and rub the butter into the flour and salt using your fingertips. When the mixture looks like fine bread crumbs, gradually add the beaten egg and start to work it in with a knife, just enough to be able to bring the dough together with your hands into a ball. Alternatively, combine the flour, salt, and butter in a food processor and gradually add the beaten egg until the pastry forms a ball. Flatten the ball of dough to form a thick disk—this will help the dough to chill through evenly. Wrap the dough in plastic wrap and chill in the fridge for 30 minutes.

Once the dough has firmed up, preheat the oven to 350°F. Remove the dough from the fridge and roll it out carefully on a lightly floured surface to about ¼-inch thick. Carefully line an 8-inch fluted tart pan with the dough, then line with a circle of parchment paper and top with baking beans. Blind-bake for 15 minutes. Remove from the oven and carefully lift out the baking beans using the paper. Set the pan aside to cool a little.

Meanwhile, prepare the filling. Melt the butter in a large nonstick frying pan and gently cook the leeks and mushrooms for about 15 minutes until softened, but not browned.

Put the cream, cheese, and eggs in a bowl. Season to taste and whisk together. Carefully spoon the mushrooms and leeks into the tart base, distributing them evenly over the bottom. Pour the cream, egg, and cheese mixture over the top and, if necessary, use the back of a spoon to even out the filling. Bake for 25 to 30 minutes until the filling is set and golden brown.

Serve hot, warm or cold with a well-dressed green salad.

SERVES 6 TO 8

FOR THE PASTRY DOUGH
1¾ cups all-purpose flour, plus extra for dusting
10 tablespoons salted butter
pinch of sea salt
1 large egg, beaten

FOR THE FILLING
2 tablespoons salted butter
2 small leeks, thinly sliced
1 pound crimini mushrooms, thinly sliced
1¼ cups heavy cream
5½ ounces smoked Cheddar (page 62), grated (about 1½ cups)
2 large eggs, plus 1 extra yolk, beaten together
salt and freshly ground black pepper

green salad, to serve

MELANZANE PARMIGIANA WITH
SMOKED MOZZARELLA

Smoky cheese and eggplant work very well together, and this classic Italian bake is a very special vegetarian main dish or a delicious side, especially as an accompaniment to roast lamb.

SERVES 4

5 teaspoons olive oil
4 large eggplant, cut crosswise into large, ½-inch thick slices
sea salt and freshly ground black pepper
2 garlic cloves, finely chopped
2 x 14-ounce cans chopped tomatoes
pinch of sugar
13 ounces smoked mozzarella (page 62), cut into ½-inch thick slices
½ cup Parmesan or strongly flavored hard cheese, grated

Preheat the oven to 350°F. Grease 2 baking pans with 2 teaspoons of the olive oil. Lay the eggplant slices on the pans in a single layer, season with salt and pepper, and bake for 20 minutes until almost tender.

Meanwhile, make the tomato sauce. Pour the remaining olive oil into a saucepan, set over medium heat, and cook the garlic gently for 2 to 3 minutes.

Drain the juice out of the cans of tomatoes (save it for another recipe), and add the tomato flesh to the garlic. Season, adding the sugar too, stir, and leave to bubble away for 10 to 15 minutes, stirring occasionally.

When the eggplant slices are baked, remove them from the oven, and arrange a single layer in the bottom of a medium-sized baking dish.

Pour in enough tomato sauce to form a layer on top of the eggplant, followed by a few slices of mozzarella. Repeat until all the eggplant, sauce, and mozzarella have been used up; I do two layers of each ingredient in an 8-inch square shallow oven dish.

Sprinkle the dish with Parmesan and bake for 35 to 40 minutes until it is golden and bubbling. Leave for 10 minutes before cutting into portions and serving.

SMOKED ROQUEFORT SALAD WITH PEARS AND WALNUTS

This classic combination of salty blue cheese, sweet juicy pears, and slightly bitter walnuts is all the better for being made with smoked cheese and caramelized walnuts (see Tip). It makes a quick, altogether delicious lunch, or a light appetizer.

SERVES 4

FOR THE DRESSING
1 teaspoon red wine vinegar
3 tablespoons extra virgin olive oil
¼ teaspoon Dijon mustard
1 teaspoon sugar
sea salt and freshly ground black pepper

FOR THE SALAD
7 ounces salad leaves—try using 3½ ounces thinly sliced chicory and 3½ ounces watercress
3½ ounces smoked blue cheese (see below), such as Roquefort, crumbled (about ¾ cup)
2 large ripe pears, thinly sliced
¾ cup walnut halves—see Tip for caramelized walnuts

Whisk all the dressing ingredients together in a small glass bowl. Taste to check the seasoning and adjust the salt and sugar, if necessary. Set aside.

Combine all the salad ingredients in a large bowl. Drizzle with the salad dressing, toss the ingredients until the leaves are just lightly glistening, and serve immediately, either on individual plates or in a large bowl in the center of the table.

TIP:

For an extra layer of flavor and crunch, try caramelizing the walnuts. Put 2 tablespoons sugar into a heavy-bottomed nonstick pan over medium heat. Leave the sugar in the pan until it melts and changes color. Swirl the liquid caramel around the pan and drop in the walnuts. Continue to swirl the walnuts in the caramel to cover them. Set the pan aside for the nuts to cool. Once cool, remove them from the pan—they will stick together—and chop them coarsely. Sprinkle over the salad just before serving.

SMOKED ROQUEFORT

Blue cheeses smoke very easily and quickly, and the smoky flavor works well with a wide range of cheeses. Do try your local blue cheese and see what you think.

MAKES 9 OUNCES

9 ounces Roquefort or other blue cheese (about 2 cups)

Place the wood in a cold smoker and light it. When it is at the correct stage (see page 11), put the Roquefort in a shallow Pyrex, glass, or ceramic dish and smoke for 30 minutes.

Wrap the smoked Roquefort well in plastic wrap and store in the fridge for up to a week.

RYGEOST

Rygeost is a creamy Danish smoked cheese. It is often made using milk and rennet, but I make a simplified version at home using cream cheese. This is not an authentic recipe, but it produces a lovely result. *Rygeost* is rarely sold outside Scandinavia, as it has a short shelf life that makes export difficult.

Try spreading this onto bread or stirring it into pasta, meat, fish, or vegetable dishes.

Start by stirring the salt into the cream cheese, then place it in a large (12-inch square) muslin or cheesecloth, tie it with string, and let it drip overnight. It could be hung on a cupboard handle with a bowl set underneath on the kitchen work surface or tied to a tap with a bowl set underneath in the sink.

Once the cream cheese has drained, put it in a shallow Pyrex, glass, or ceramic dish. Smooth out the top, so that the cheese is leveled out and even, and sprinkle with the caraway seeds. Loosely cover the dish with muslin or cheesecloth.

Place the wood in a cold smoker and light it. When it is at the correct stage (see page 11), add the cheese and smoke for 2 hours.

Tightly wrap the *rygeost* (in its dish) in plastic wrap and store in the fridge for up to a week.

MAKES **18** OUNCES

2 teaspoons sea salt
1 pound full-fat cream cheese
2 teaspoons caraway seeds

TROUT WITH LEEKS, RYGEOST, AND DILL

This Danish-inspired dish really encapsulates the flavors of Scandinavia: fresh fish, smoked cheese, and fresh anisey dill. It is wonderful served warm as a main course with some rye bread on the side, or as a cold salad.

Start by poaching the trout. Place the fillets skin-side down in a shallow-sided frying pan. Cover with water, bring to a boil, turn the heat off, and leave the fish to sit in the water for 7 minutes.

Meanwhile, melt the butter in a saucepan. Add the leeks and sauté for 10 minutes until soft and translucent. Add lemon juice to taste, the *rygeost*, salt and pepper, and caraway seeds. Gently stir over medium heat to warm the *rygeost* and stir it through the leeks to make a creamy sauce.

Remove the trout from the pan after 7 minutes. Pat the fillets dry with paper towels, remove the skin, and break up the trout into large flakes.

Serve the leeks topped with flaked trout and sprinkled with plenty of fresh dill. Serve warm or cold.

SERVES 2 AS A MAIN COURSE OR 4 AS AN APPETIZER

2 trout, filleted
1 tablespoon salted butter
2 fresh leeks, thinly sliced on an angle
juice of ½ to 1 lemon, to taste
3½ ounces *rygeost* (page 69)
sea salt and freshly ground black pepper
1 teaspoon caraway seeds
2 tablespoons chopped fresh dill fronds

ORECCHIETTE BAKED WITH SQUASH, SMOKED RICOTTA, AND SAGE

An all-Italian vegetarian supper dish that is colorful and comforting at the same time. With smoked ricotta ready in your fridge, this will quickly become a midweek favorite, wonderfully warming on a cold day, and a complete meal in one dish.

2½ cups butternut squash, peeled and cut into ½-inch cubes
3 tablespoons salted butter
3 tablespoons extra virgin olive oil
12 ounces cherry tomatoes
20 sage leaves
2 teaspoons cumin seeds
pinch of red pepper flakes
sea salt and freshly ground black pepper
9 ounces orecchiette pasta
1 cup smoked ricotta (page 62)
1 cup Parmesan, grated

Preheat the oven to 350°F.

Put the cubed squash in a large nonstick frying pan over medium to high heat and add the butter and oil. Stir-fry for about 15 minutes to gently soften. Next, add the tomatoes, sage, cumin, and pepper flakes and season well.

Next cook the pasta. Bring a large saucepan of salted water to a boil. Cook the orecchiette for a minute or two less than the package instructions indicate so that the pasta is not overcooked in the final dish. Drain.

Stir the pasta through the squash and tomatoes, and transfer to a large ovenproof baking dish—an 8 x 12-inch shallow-sided dish is ideal. Dot the ricotta evenly over the top of the dish, followed by the Parmesan.

Bake for 30 to 40 minutes until the squash is tender and the cheese is melted, golden, and bubbling. Serve hot. Any leftovers will keep for a couple of days, covered, in the fridge.

BARBECUED LOBSTER WITH SMOKED BUTTER

Fresh lobster is always a real treat but the sweet flesh tastes particularly sublime when cooked with smoked butter. It makes a really special centerpiece for a barbecue or summer supper, enjoyed al fresco. I like the flavor of cooking the lobster over oak and hickory wood charcoal on the Big Green Egg here.

SERVES 4

2 cooked lobsters
7 tablespoons smoked butter (see below)
sea salt and freshly ground black pepper
2 lemons, cut into wedges, to serve

Preheat the grill until very hot.

Split the cooked lobsters in half lengthwise. It is easiest to do this with a large chopping knife by inserting the point of the knife in the middle of the tail, working back carefully toward the head in one, careful slice.

Melt the smoked butter in a pan and brush a little over the flesh of the lobster. Set the remaining melted butter aside, keeping it warm.

Grill, cut-side down, for about 5 minutes until the meat is piping hot and lightly chargrilled.

Remove the lobster from the grill, remove the meat from the shell, and immediately drop it into the warm melted butter. Toss the lobster in the butter, season with salt and pepper, and serve in warm bowls, with lemon wedges on the side.

Enjoy warm, either on its own with some excellent bread to mop up the smoked butter, with a crisp, green salad, or even, for the ultimate indulgence, spooned on to a juicy steak.

SMOKED BUTTER

This is a great place to start if you haven't smoked anything before. It's quick, easy, and so delicious. Try melting smoked butter on steamed vegetables, grilled steaks, and even sweet treats, such as chocolate brownies, for an extra dimension of smoky flavor.

MAKES 16 TABLESPOONS

16 tablespoons (2 sticks) salted butter

Set up the cold smoker using a wood of your choice and light it. Put the butter in a heatproof, nonmetallic dish. When the smoker is at the correct stage (see page 11), with a thick cloud of smoke appearing in the cold chamber, add the butter and smoke for 30 minutes.

Remove the butter, wrap well, and store in the fridge. Leave it for 24 hours before eating.

The smoked butter will keep for up to a month in the fridge.

SMOKED BUTTER FUDGE

Smoky fudge is unusual, but really delicious. I think it is best enjoyed outdoors, after a barbecue or as a campfire treat. The smokiness counters the intense sweetness well, and this is my favorite kind of fudge—soft, smooth, and creamy.

Line a shallow 8 x 12-inch pan with nonstick parchment paper. Set aside.

Put the butter, condensed milk, whole milk, corn syrup, and sugar in a large, heavy-bottomed saucepan. Heat over low heat, stirring regularly, until the sugar has completely dissolved.

Increase the heat and bring the fudge to a boil. When it reaches boiling point, set the timer and boil for 12 minutes. It should reach the soft-ball stage now. To test, carefully remove a teaspoonful of the mixture and drop it into a glass of very cold water. It should quickly form a soft, smooth ball. If the fudge is too runny still, boil for another 2 minutes and test again. Don't boil for much longer, though, as it will be too firm.

Remove the pan from the heat, stir in the vanilla extract and sea salt, and set aside to cool for 10 minutes. Transfer the fudge to a stand mixer with a whisk attachment and beat for 5 minutes until thickened and the fudge has lost its sheen. You can also beat the fudge by hand in a very large mixing bowl with a wooden spoon if you don't have a stand mixer. It is hard work though!

Transfer the fudge to the prepared pan. Smooth the top using a offset spatula, cover with plastic wrap, and put in the fridge to firm up for at least 4 hours. Carefully cut into squares. Keep in the fridge or an airtight lidded container for a couple of weeks.

MAKES ABOUT 60 SQUARES

16 tablespoons (2 sticks) smoked salted butter (page 77)
1 x 14-ounce can condensed milk
¾ cup whole milk
4 teaspoons corn syrup
3½ cups granulated cane sugar
3 teaspoons vanilla extract
1 heaping teaspoon sea salt

MEAT

HOMEMADE BACON

Curing and smoking your own bacon takes time but it is so rewarding. It also makes a very special gift—if you can bear to part with it! This recipe uses the dry curing method, which draws water from the bacon. If you'd like to make meatier, Canadian-style bacon, you can use pork tenderloin instead of pork belly.

Makes about 4½ pounds

1 large piece of pork belly or pork tenderloin, weighing about 4½ pounds
¼ cup sea salt

Rub the meat all over with the salt and place in a large, shallow Pyrex, glass, or ceramic dish, on a rack, to allow the liquid that will be drawn from the meat to drain away. Pour off the liquid as soon as it collects in the bottom of the dish.

Cover the dish and leave the bacon to salt for 2 days in the fridge.

Once the bacon is salted, rinse the meat well and dry it thoroughly with paper towels. If it still feels a bit damp, it can be returned to the fridge and left for 12 hours to dry further before smoking. Cold smoke your bacon for 24 hours (see page 16). It can be hung on a butcher's hook or just placed directly on the rack or on top of the rack in a dish.

Your bacon can be thinly or thickly sliced and fried or broiled. You can slice it then wrap it, or keep in a single piece and slice when required. It will keep in the fridge for about a week, well wrapped.

MAPLE AND BROWN SUGAR CURED BACON

Add ¼ cup of maple syrup and ¼ cup of brown sugar to the salt in the above recipe.

SMOKED BACON JAM WITH MAPLE AND WHISKEY

This bacon jam combines so many delicious flavors—maple syrup, coffee, whiskey—to make an irresistible savory, sweet, and sticky spread. Try it spread on hot toast, with eggs at breakfast time, spread on burgers, or with cheese. It's a revelation.

Start by gently warming the oil in a large nonstick frying pan. Add the chopped bacon, garlic, onion, and chile and cook over medium heat for about 10 minutes until fragrant and sweet. Add the remaining ingredients and slowly cook for about an hour until the jam is thick, sticky, and caramelized. Once it is a soft spreading consistency, remove from the heat and let cool.

Once the jam is cooled, it will have thickened a little more. If you have a food processor, just give the jam an extra blitz quickly, to create a slightly smoother texture. This can also be achieved by chopping the ingredients very, very finely.

Transfer to a 16-ounce sterilized, lidded jar and store in the fridge where it will keep, sealed, for a month. Once opened, consume within 3 weeks.

MAKES 1 x 16-OUNCE JAR

2 teaspoons olive oil
1¼ pounds smoked bacon (page 80), finely chopped
4 garlic cloves, crushed
1 medium red onion, finely chopped
1 red chile, seeded and finely chopped
½ cup maple syrup
2 teaspoons red wine vinegar
2 teaspoons cider vinegar
⅔ cup strong, freshly made coffee
½ cup whiskey

HOT-SMOKED DUCK BREASTS

Duck lends itself very well to smoky flavors. Hot smoking duck breasts in a stovetop smoker is a quick method and transforms the meat into something incredibly special. Smoked duck breasts are especially good served warm, or indeed hot. You can also enjoy them cold but I prefer them warm or hot.

MAKES 4

FOR THE CURE
4 duck breasts, skin on
2 tablespoons demerara sugar
1½ tablespoons salt

1½ tablespoons hickory, cedar, or apple wood chips

TIP:

For extra crispy skin, score the skin at ½-inch internals using a small, sharp knife before pan-frying or baking

Dry the duck breasts using paper towels. Make the cure by mixing together the sugar and salt, and rub this over the meat. Put the breasts in a shallow Pyrex, glass, or ceramic dish or bowl, cover, and transfer to the fridge for at least 30 minutes or up to 1 hour, if possible.

Just before you are ready to smoke the meat, rinse off the cure and dry again thoroughly.

Place the wood chips in the center of a stovetop hot smoker (see page 11). Add the duck breasts, cover, and smoke for 30 minutes.

Meanwhile, preheat the oven to 350°F if you plan to oven bake the duck.

When the duck breasts are smoked, either pan-fry them, skin-side down, over medium heat until cooked and the skin is crisp (turning over for the last couple of minutes of cooking) or transfer them to a large nonstick baking pan and bake for 15 to 20 minutes.

SMOKED CHICKEN BREASTS

Smoked chicken breast is especially good paired with sweet and spicy ingredients. You can smoke game birds in this way, although smaller breasts of say partridge or grouse will smoke more quickly. Pheasant should take roughly the same amount of time as chicken.

You can also make a cure for the chicken using sugar, herbs, and spices if you wish to introduce some additional flavors to your smoked chicken.

Rub the salt into the chicken breasts, put in a Pyrex, glass, or ceramic dish or bowl, cover, and transfer to the fridge for anywhere from 30 minutes to 2 hours.

Remove from the fridge and rinse well under cold running water. Dry the chicken thoroughly with paper towels and set on a plate ready to smoke.

Place the wood chips in the center of a hot smoker. When it is at the correct stage (page 11), place the chicken breasts on the rack and smoke for 20 minutes. They should take on a more ocher shade and release some liquid.

The chicken breasts can be pan-fried to cook them through, or roasted in the oven at 350°F for 15 to 20 minutes until the skin is crisp and the meat is fully cooked.

To check the chicken is cooked, insert the tip of a sharp knife into the thickest part of the breast and ensure the juices run clear and that the meat is no longer pink or translucent.

MAKES 4

4 chicken breasts, skin on
2 teaspoons sea salt

2 tablespoons apple wood chips or shavings

SMOKED DUCK SALAD WITH ORANGE, POMEGRANATE, AND PECANS

Smoked duck breasts are very deeply flavored and here the rich meat is cut through with the freshness of orange and pomegranate.
I like this salad best when the duck is added to the salad warm, having just been smoked and pan-fried.

Serves 6

½ cup pecans
3 ounces salad leaves, such as watercress
seeds of ½ pomegranate
1 large orange, zested and segmented over a small bowl to catch 3 tablespoons juice
½ cup extra virgin olive oil
sea salt and freshly ground black pepper
4 hot-smoked duck breasts (page 84), cut into ½-inch thick slices

Preheat the oven to 350°F.

Spread out the pecans on a nonstick baking pan—no need to use any oil—and roast them for 8 to 10 minutes until lightly toasted. Set aside to cool.

Put the salad leaves in a large bowl and add the pomegranate seeds and orange segments.

Make a dressing by whisking the orange juice, zest, and oil together. Season with salt and pepper. Pour this over the salad leaves and toss together well. Taste to check the seasoning. Serve immediately, topped with the slices of duck and roasted pecans.

SMOKED CHICKEN AND CHORIZO PAELLA

This recipe for paella is my all-time favorite, featuring a powerful trio of smoked ingredients: chicken, paprika, and chorizo. It is a great recipe to make when feeding a crowd—a generous, one-pot feast that requires surprisingly little time and attention to prepare. This is a particularly pleasing recipe for anyone who loves the idea of paella but isn't keen on seafood. You don't need a paella pan: a large, shallow-sided pan or Dutch oven with a lid will work fine.

Heat the oil in a large, shallow-sided pan or a lidded Dutch oven. Add the fresh and dried chorizo and cook very gently until the fat is released.

Add the onion and cook for about 10 minutes until translucent, then add the garlic and continue to cook over low heat until fragrant. Use a slotted spoon to remove the chorizo, onion, and garlic and set aside, keeping the oil in the pan.

Increase the heat and add the chicken. Cook for 5 to 10 minutes until lightly browned on all sides then reduce the heat and return the chorizo, onion, and garlic to the pan. Stir in the saffron, red pepper flakes, paprika, and tomatoes.

Add the rice, hot stock, and lemon juice and bring to a boil. Reduce the heat right down, cover with the lid, and cook for 20 to 30 minutes, stirring gently very occasionally, until the rice and chicken are cooked and the stock has been absorbed.

Take the pan to the table to serve, topping the paella with a generous sprinkling of chopped flat-leaf parsley and plenty of fresh lemon wedges on the side.

SERVES 6 TO 8

1 tablespoon olive oil
7 ounces fresh cooking chorizo, cut into ¼-inch thick slices
7 ounces dried chorizo sausage, cut into ¼-inch thick slices
1 large white onion, halved and cut into ⅛-inch thick slices
4 garlic cloves, chopped
4 hot-smoked chicken breasts (page 85), skin removed and cut into large chunks
pinch of saffron
1 teaspoon red pepper flakes
1 tablespoon smoked paprika
1 x 14-ounce can chopped tomatoes
2 cups paella rice, such as calasparra or bomba
1 quart hot chicken stock
1 tablespoon lemon juice
fresh flat-leaf parsley and lemon wedges, to serve

SMOKED CHICKEN SALAD WITH
MANGO, CHILE, AND FRESH HERBS

This salad is vibrant and fresh, combining punchy flavors and contrasting textures. Smoked chicken breasts add another layer of interest to the mix.

SERVES 4

¼ cup unsalted shelled cashews or pistachios
4 chicken breasts, apple wood smoked (page 85), cut widthwise into ½-inch thick slices
1 large mango, peeled, pitted, and cut into ½-inch cubes
3 ounces salad leaves
½ cup fresh cilantro leaves, coarsely chopped
½ cup fresh mint leaves, coarsely chopped
sea salt

FOR THE DRESSING
1 teaspoon honey
5 tablespoons extra virgin olive oil
1 tablespoon lemon juice
1 red chile, seeded and finely chopped

Preheat the oven to 350°F.

Spread out the nuts on a nonstick baking pan and roast for 5 to 8 minutes until lightly golden. Remove from the oven and set aside to cool.

Put the dressing ingredients in a bowl and whisk to combine. Set aside.

Add all the salad ingredients to a large serving bowl. Pour over the dressing and sprinkle with the toasted nuts. Gently toss to combine everything. Taste and season with sea salt if required. Serve immediately.

SWISS CHALET POTATOES

This is a lovely potato dish that works so well with baked ham. It makes an easy and different side and is delicious served with roasted meat or casseroles.

Put the potatoes in a large pan of water and bring to a boil. Cook until tender, drain, and set aside. Preheat the oven to 400°F

Put all the remaining ingredients in a bowl and mix well.

Transfer the potatoes into a large ovenproof dish approximately 8 x 8-inch or slightly smaller works. Carefully pour the creamy cheesy mixture evenly over the potatoes. Bake for 20 to 30 minutes until the cheese is bubbling and a light golden brown. Serve immediately.

SERVES 6

1¾ pounds large Russet potatoes, peeled and
  cut into 1¼-inch chunks
1¼ cups grated Gruyère
¾ cup heavy cream
1 teaspoon Dijon mustard
sea salt and freshly ground black pepper

SPICE-GLAZED SMOKED HAM

This is a superb way to cook a ham, and is comparatively quick and easy, too. A whole cooked ham is a gorgeous piece of meat to serve as a centerpiece when feeding a crowd or hosting a special occasion, not just at Christmas. A top-quality ham is unbeatable, and I promise you, this will wow your guests.

Make sure you buy an unsmoked ham, which will have already been brined.

Serves 12

1 unsmoked ham, weighing 5½ to 6½ pounds

For the glaze
1 cup light brown sugar
½ teaspoon ground nutmeg
½ teaspoon ground cinnamon
½ teaspoon allspice
3 teaspoons Dijon mustard
¼ cup Calvados or whiskey

2 tablespoons apple, oak, or birch wood chips or shavings

Place the ham in a large saucepan or stockpot and cover fully with cold water. Cover with a lid and bring to a boil. Once the water boils, completely drain the pan and pour cold water in, keeping the ham in the pan. Repeat this process several times—the water will be rather murky and you may notice some dark foam. The water will gradually become clearer after about five or six rounds of filling and draining.

Fill the pan up once again, cover, and bring to a boil. Cook the ham for 2 hours, keeping the pan topped off with water if the level drops. Check if the meat is cooked by inserting a metal skewer deep into the flesh. Lift the skewer and if the meat slides off back into the pan immediately, then it will be nice and tender. If you notice some resistance and the ham clings to the skewer, then it will need cooking for longer. Continue to boil for another 20 minutes and test again. It may take 2½ to 3 hours to become tender.

When the ham is cooked, pour off the water from the pan and leave the ham to dry naturally, which will take about 30 minutes.

Meanwhile, make up the glaze by mixing all the ingredients together to form a thick paste. Set aside.

When you are ready to smoke the ham, preheat the hot smoker to 200°F (see page 11). Place the ham on a large metal pan and pour the glaze over the meat. Rub the glaze all over the meat and skin and place in the hot smoker, reserving any excess marinade. Smoke for 1 to 2 hours, depending on how smoky you like the meat to taste. The flesh will become firmer the longer it is smoked. Every 30 minutes, brush more of the reserved marinade over the meat, cover, and continue smoking.

Serve the ham immediately with Swiss Chalet Potatoes (page 91) or let cool and serve cold.

SMOKED HAM HOCK

Cooking and smoking whole ham hocks is one of the most delicious ways to use this economical and flavorful cut. Ham hocks are available in most butchers; you might just need to give the butcher a few days' notice.

The amount of meat a ham hock yields does vary, but I found there to be an average of 6 ounces per hock, when well prepared, cutting out all the nice bits. The bones can be simmered to make an excellent stock, or a traditional ham and pea soup using split peas. Do cut off the fat, remove the skin, and render it. Store it in a container and use it for frying and cooking.

MAKES ABOUT 1½ POUNDS HAM

4 good-quality ham hocks, skin on

2 tablespoons oak or apple wood chips or shavings

Place the ham hocks in a large saucepan or stockpot and cover fully with cold water. If you don't have a pan large enough, use a couple of pans—just make sure the hocks are all submerged.

Cover and bring to a boil. Once the water boils, completely drain the pan. Pour cold water into the pan, keeping the ham hocks in the pan. The water will be rather murky and you may notice some dark foam. Pour the water off and repeat. The water will gradually become clearer after about five or six rounds of filling and draining. Fill the pan up once again, cover, and bring to a boil. Cook the hocks for 2 hours, keeping the pan topped off with water, if the level drops. You can tell if the ham is cooked by inserting a metal skewer deep into the flesh. Lift the skewer, while inserted into the meat. If the hock slides off back into the pan immediately, then it will be nice and tender. If you notice some resistance and the hock clings to the skewer, then it will need cooking for longer. Continue to boil for another 20 minutes and test again. Some tough hocks may take 2½ to 3 hours to become tender.

When the hocks are cooked, drain them and leave them to dry naturally. Leave them to sit for at least 30 minutes or up to an hour, if you have time.

When you are ready to smoke the hocks, preheat the hot smoker (see page 11). When the hocks are dry, place them in the hot smoker and smoke for 1 to 2 hours, depending on how smoky you would like the hock to taste. The flesh does become firmer the longer it is smoked; so do bear this in mind. Once the ham hocks are smoked, the skin and fat can be removed and the meat shredded. It will keep in the fridge for up to 5 days.

SMOKED HAM HOCK CROQUETAS

Croquetas are one of the most delicious ways to enjoy smoked ham hock. I lived in Spain for a time, which is where I first learned to make them. *Croquetas* (see photo on pages 96–97), or croquettes, are delectable crispy morsels that should be served warm so that their creamy center is unctuous and silky. They are a vehicle for many flavors, including chicken, tuna, and shrimp, but ham is the most traditional option. Sometimes *croquetas* are made with Serrano ham in Spain, but I prefer smoked ham hock, which is softer in texture, but still deeply flavorful. Although they require a little time to make, they are a real treat. They are delicious served as a canapé with a light beer or cava, or as part of a tapas spread.

MAKES 50 CROQUETAS

3 tablespoons olive oil
1 leek or ½ small white onion, very finely chopped
1 cup all-purpose flour
3 cups whole milk
10½ ounces ham hock (page 94), very finely chopped (about 2 cups)
pinch of nutmeg
¾ cup aged Cheddar, grated
olive or sunflower oil, for frying

FOR THE COATING
½ cup all-purpose flour
2 large eggs, beaten
3 cups dried white bread crumbs

Heat the olive oil in a deep heavy-bottomed pan over medium heat. Add the leek, reduce the heat, and cook for 5 to 10 minutes until it turns translucent. Stir in the flour and cook for 5 minutes, stirring constantly.

Meanwhile, warm the milk and add it to the pan, a ladleful at a time. Remove the mixture from the heat and blend it until smooth, using an immersion blender.

Add the ham and the nutmeg to the pan. Return the mixture to the heat and keep stirring it until you have a thick béchamel sauce. Now add the grated Cheddar. Stir and pour into a shallow dish. Let cool for at least 4 hours or overnight if you prefer. The béchamel needs to be very thick and firm to retain its shape when it cooks.

To coat and fry the *croquetas* line up three dishes: put the flour in the first, beaten egg in the second, and bread crumbs in the third. Pick up a tablespoonful of the mixture (it must be firm to do this—if it is not, return it to the fridge for another hour or two) and use your hands to mold it into a cylinder shape. Place them on a baking pan lined with nonstick parchment paper. Keep doing this until you've used up all of the mixture.

Coat each croqueta first in flour, then in egg, and finally in bread crumbs. Put them in the fridge for an hour so that they become firm. They are even better if you freeze them—they will last up to 3 months in the freezer. (You can fry them from frozen—allow 3 minutes more cooking.)

Fry the *croquetas* in small batches in lots of oil in a small deep-sided frying pan for 4 to 5 minutes until they are a rich golden brown. (Or a deep-fat fryer is perfect, if you have one.) Remove with a slotted spoon and drain them on paper towels before serving warm.

The croquetas will be so hot when they come out the fryer, they will remain hot for 10 minutes or so before serving. But if you need to keep them hot for longer, put them on a large nonstick baking pan in the oven at 175°F until you are ready to serve them. They won't stay hot for longer than 30 minutes before getting a bit soggy, so it's best to fry them in batches as close to serving time as possible.

SMOKED SAUSAGES

You can smoke almost all kinds of sausages, but you should smoke fresh, rather than dried, ones. A stovetop hot smoker will work perfectly here and apple or oak pairs very nicely with pork.

Place the wood in a hot smoker. When it is at the correct stage (see page 11), add the sausages and smoke for 20 minutes. They should have a lightly golden or brown tinge and be just starting to release a little liquid.

Meanwhile, preheat the oven to 350°F or preheat the broiler or barbecue if using.

Once the sausages are smoked, place them on a large nonstick baking pan and roast for 15 to 20 minutes until they are sizzling and cooked through and the skins are a rich brown.

MAKES 8 SMOKED SAUSAGES

8 fresh sausages

PØLSE

Serves 6

12 good-quality pork sausages
12 Hot dog buns (see below)
Ristede løg (see below)

To serve
Celeriac and caper remoulade (page 41),
    Pickled Cucumber (page 20), or other
    sauces and pickles of your choice

Danish hot dogs are a real national staple, and I tried my first-ever hot dog in Denmark. Many are made using frankfurter sausages, which are usually smoked, but they are also really good made with great-quality fresh pork sausages, which can be hot smoked and finished on the grill to brown the skins a little. Frankfurter sausages just need warming through—they don't cook well under a broiler or on a grill as the skins split open very easily. Use any combination of accompaniments you fancy—the traditional Danish options are *ristede løg* (crispy onions), mustard, remoulade, pickles, or thinly sliced gherkins and perhaps some ketchup.

Hot smoke the sausages (see page 99) and finish them by broiling or barbecuing until they are cooked through, sizzling, and have crispy skins.

Serve the sausages in buns, split lengthwise, with crispy onions and your favorite sauces.

HOT DOG BUNS

Makes 12 large rolls

8 cups bread flour, plus extra for dusting
1¼ tablespoons fast-acting dried yeast
2 teaspoons sea salt
3 cups whole milk
7 tablespoons salted butter
oil, for greasing
1 large egg, beaten

Put the flour, yeast, and salt in the bowl of a stand mixer or large bowl and stir to combine evenly.

Pour the milk into a saucepan and add the butter. Warm gently so that the butter melts but do not allow the milk to become warmer than lukewarm temperature. Once the butter has melted, slowly pour the milk into the flour and stir to form a sticky dough. Knead for 10 minutes, either by hand or in a stand mixer using the dough hook.

Put the dough into an oiled bowl, cover the bowl with plastic wrap, and let the dough rise for 1 to 2 hours until it has doubled in size.

Punch down the dough and shape into 12 long rolls. Put on a lightly floured baking sheet, cover the bread with a cloth, and let it rise until doubled in size again. Now preheat the oven to 375°F.

When you're ready to bake, glaze the rolls with the egg and bake for 25 minutes. The rolls are ready when they are golden brown and sound hollow when the base is rapped with your knuckles. Place the rolls on a wire rack to cool fully.

RISTEDE LØG

serves 6

2 large white onions, very thinly sliced
2 tablespoons sunflower oil or duck fat
sea salt

Simply cook the onions gently in hot oil or duck fat until very crispy. Season well. Once cooked, let them drain briefly on some paper towels to blot any excess oil before serving.

SMOKED MERGUEZ

Merguez sausage is a richly spiced sausage originating from North Africa and traditionally made by Bedouins. *Merguez* is also very popular in France and the Middle East. It is mostly made using a mixture of lamb and beef, with harissa, chile, paprika, fennel, aniseed, cumin, cinnamon, sumac, lemon, and garlic to flavor the meat. *Merguez* sausage is not hard to find; I order mine online. A good butcher should be able to point you in the right direction, or if you are really lucky, make some for you.

As good as *merguez* is, I find them irresistible smoked. The subtle yet distinctive flavor smoking imparts heightens the complex flavors of the *merguez*. Hickory wood is a wonderful wood to use here and for the best flavor and texture, hot smoke the sausages and finish them off in the oven for sizzling skins. Superb served as part of a barbecue, or even as an informal appetizer with drinks.

MAKES 8 SMOKED SAUSAGES

8 *merguez* sausages

1½ teaspoons hickory wood

Put the hickory wood in a hot smoker. When it is at the correct stage (see page 11), add the *merguez* and smoke for 20 minutes. They should be quite smoky and just starting to sweat.

Meanwhile, preheat the oven to 350°F or light the grill.

Once the sausages are smoked, place them on a large nonstick baking pan and roast for 15 to 20 minutes until they are cooked through, sizzling, and the skins are a rich brown. Grill for 10 to 20 minutes, depending on the temperature and thickness of the sausages.

KIELBASA

Kielbasa are Polish sausages. There are actually several different types of *kielbasa*, including white sausages, blood sausages, and *kabanossi*, which are made using beef and pork.

This is my version of the most widely found type of *kielbasa*—a pork sausage flavored with paprika and garlic. They are really delicious when smoked.

Start by preparing the sausage casings by rinsing them very well in fresh, cold water. Set them aside.

Put the pork in a bowl, add the additional ingredients, and mix together. Transfer everything to a food processor and process to create a smooth mixture.

Fill the sausage casings with the sausage meat by piping the meat in and tying a knot in each end. You should have 6 to 8 sausages, which will keep for 5 days in the fridge, well wrapped.

Place the wood in a hot smoker. When it is at the correct stage (see page 11), add the sausages and smoke for 20 minutes. The skins should be lightly browned, but still soft, and just starting to release a little liquid.

Meanwhile, preheat the oven to 350°F or light the grill.

Once the sausages are smoked, place them on a large nonstick baking pan and roast for 15 to 20 minutes until they are cooked through, sizzling, and the skins are a rich brown. Cook on the grill for about 15 minutes.

SERVES 6

3 to 5 feet natural sausage casings (this allows enough room to maneuver)
1¼ pounds pork shoulder, cut into chunks
2 teaspoons sea salt
generous grind black pepper
2 teaspoons paprika
½ teaspoon chile powder
5 garlic cloves, crushed
½ teaspoon caraway seeds

SMOKED MERGUEZ SALAD WITH ORANGE, WATERCRESS, AND HONEY-SPICED ALMONDS

Freshly hot smoked *merguez* sausages work superbly in this salad. To transform this into more substantial fare—an excellent meal for a larger group to share—serve the sausages and salad in separate bowls, with another large bowl filled with hot, fluffy couscous, some olive oil, and perhaps a few drops of orange blossom water stirred through.

First prepare the almonds by warming the olive oil, honey, paprika, and cumin in a small frying pan. Add the almonds and stir over the heat to coat the nuts and continue to cook for about 5 minutes. The honey and spices will thicken, caramelize, and start to bubble. When this stage is reached, remove the almonds from the heat and set aside to cool, giving them the occasional prod to ensure they don't stick together. The almonds will be coated in a sticky, spicy caramel, but won't be too crisp or browned.

Make the dressing. Take a large bowl and whisk together the honey, olive oil, and orange zest and juice, then stir in the chopped herbs and orange segments. Add the sausages and watercress, ensuring the salad is evenly dressed. The sausages can be used whole or cut into bite-sized chunks according to taste. Finally, stir in the almonds and serve immediately.

SERVES 4

FOR THE HONEY-SPICED ALMONDS
½ teaspoon olive oil
1 tablespoon honey
pinch of paprika
pinch of ground cumin
⅓ cup whole blanched almonds

FOR THE DRESSING
½ teaspoon honey
¼ cup extra virgin olive oil
zest and juice of 1 large orange
2 tablespoons chopped fresh flat-leaf
    parsley
2 tablespoons chopped fresh mint

FOR THE SAUSAGES AND SALAD
1 orange, segmented
8 smoked and cooked *merguez* sausages
    (page 103), warm
1 large bunch of fresh watercress, about
    5½ ounces

SMOKED BEEF CHEEKS

Beef cheek is a wonderful inexpensive cut. It requires slow cooking, but the result is the most delicious, lean, meltingly tender meat. Smoking beef cheek adds another layer of flavor that works very well in slow-cooked dishes.

Rub the salt into the beef and put in a shallow Pyrex, glass, or ceramic dish, cover, and transfer to the fridge for between 30 minutes and 2 hours.

Remove from the fridge and rinse them well under cold running water. Dry them thoroughly on paper towels and set on a plate ready to smoke.

Place the wood in a hot smoker. When it is at the correct stage (see page 11), place the cheeks on the rack and smoke for 20 minutes. They will shrink a little as they smoke.

The cheeks can be pan-fried in a little olive oil to seal them and then added, whole, to a Dutch oven and cooked for at least 3 hours.

MAKES 4 SMOKED BEEF CHEEKS

4 teaspoons sea salt
4 whole beef cheeks

2 tablespoons oak or mesquite wood chips
  or shavings

BRAISED SMOKED BEEF CHEEKS WITH GREMOLATA

This is a stunning and satisfying dish. The beef cheeks are slow cooked until they fall apart in a rich and intensely flavored sauce. The meat is served sprinkled with gremolata—a dry mixture of herbs, citrus zest, and raw garlic, which elevates the dish to something special.

Try using half smoked, half unsmoked beef for a subtle but interesting flavor.

Heat the oil in a large Dutch oven over medium heat. Brown the beef cheeks then add the crushed garlic. Cook for about 5 minutes until the garlic is translucent, then add the remaining ingredients. Bring to a simmer, cover, and cook for 3 hours. Season to taste.

To make the gremolata, finely chop the parsley, zest the lemons, finely grate the garlic, then mix together. To serve, sprinkle the gremolata over the cooked beef cheeks. Buttery mashed potatoes and stir-fried cavolo nero make superb accompaniments.

SERVES 4 TO 6

3 tablespoons olive oil
2¼ pounds smoked beef cheeks—about
  3 cheeks (see above)
8 garlic cloves, crushed
1 x 14-ounce can tomatoes
1 quart beef stock
¾ cup balsamic vinegar
2 large sprigs fresh rosemary
3 large sprigs fresh thyme
1 bay leaf
salt and freshly ground black pepper
mashed potatoes and cavolo nero, to serve

FOR THE GREMOLATA
handful of fresh flat-leaf parsley, stalks
  removed
2 organic lemons
2 garlic cloves, peeled

SMOKED PORK BELLY

Pork belly is a relatively inexpensive cut but the meat is soft and tender. Try adding chunks of smoked pork belly to a cassoulet, use it to make a Cantonese *char siu*, or, if you have a really meaty piece, turn it into smoked pulled pork.

SERVES 4

¼ cup sea salt
1 piece of pork belly, weighing about
   2¼ pounds

Rub the salt into the pork and set in a large, shallow Pyrex, glass, or ceramic dish on a rack, to allow the liquid that will be drawn from the meat to drain. Pour out the liquid as soon as it collects in the bottom of the dish.

Leave the meat to salt for 2 days, well covered, in the fridge.

Once the meat is salted, rinse well and dry it thoroughly with paper towels. Cold smoke the belly piece for 24 hours (see page 16).

The pork will keep, well wrapped, for up to a week in the fridge before it needs cooking.

FEIJOADA

1 tablespoon olive oil
1 large white onion, chopped
1 red chile, seeded and finely chopped
1¼ pounds smoked pork belly (see above),
   cut into ¾-inch slices
10½ ounces cooking chorizo, cut into
   ½-inch slices
7 ounces smoked bacon (page 80), cut into
   ¼ to ½-inch chunks
1 x 14-ounce can black beans, drained
   and rinsed
½ teaspoon fresh thyme leaves
2 teaspoons paprika
1 teaspoon red wine vinegar
2 cups chicken stock
rice, to serve

This Brazilian pork and bean stew contains a delicious combination of smoked ingredients, including smoked paprika in the chorizo. It has real depth of flavor, and is excellent served with rice and maybe some slices of orange on the side. This is a great dish to make if you have a piece of smoked bacon, rather than using presliced, although store-bought, sliced bacon does work well.

Heat the oil in a large, heavy-bottomed pan over medium heat. Add the onion and cook for 5 to 10 minutes until softened. Add the chile, pork belly, chorizo, and bacon and cook for about 5 minutes until the pork is lightly browned. Add the remaining ingredients, then bring to simmering point. Cook for 2 to 3 hours until the sauce is rich and the meat is meltingly tender. Serve with rice if you wish.

SMOKED BEEF RIBS

Beef ribs, also sold as short ribs, are the rack of ribs cut from the flank, or the middle of the animal, rather than from the back. They are really meaty and the flesh just melts in the mouth after a long, slow cook. Braising beef ribs works especially well.

There are several ways in which beef ribs can be smoked and prepared—and I cannot urge you strongly enough to try my recipe for Asian spiced smoked beef ribs. Beef ribs are a great cut to experiment with—they can be cured with salt and sugar before smoking, or—for a quick and easy version—simply dried fully, seasoned with salt and pepper and hot smoked for about 2 hours to impart a subtle, delicious smokiness, then cut into generous chunks and braised or casseroled.

To hot smoke 6 ribs, simply mix 2 tablespoons of sea salt with 2 tablespoons of superfine sugar and rub onto the ribs. Set aside in the fridge to cure for at least 2 hours. Pat the meat dry with paper towels once cured (or wash the cure off if you prefer) and hot smoke for at least 2 hours (see page 11). If the smoker runs hot then they will be ready to eat, otherwise they can be finished off in the oven at 350°F for about 20 minutes.

ASIAN-SPICED SMOKED BEEF RIBS

These dark, sticky ribs are a real treat. Rice wine and soy sauce combine to make a delicious sauce in which the ribs are briefly cooked with warm spices before hot smoking. You can ask a butcher to cut the ribs for you, which makes the dish easy to prepare.

Put the rice wine, soy sauce, sugar, vinegar, salt, cardamom, ginger, and ketchup in a large saucepan over low heat. Whisk briefly to combine all the ingredients together. Add the beef rib chunks and gently simmer, covered, for 45 minutes.

Remove the beef from the pan and set aside on a plate while you preheat the hot smoker.

Meanwhile, return the pan to the heat, without the beef, and boil steadily, until the sauce has reduced until thick and slightly sticky.

When the hot smoker is ready (see page 11), place the ribs in and smoke for 30 to 45 minutes. Brush the meat every 5 to 10 minutes with the sticky marinade, and turn the meat regularly.

Once the ribs are hot, lightly smoked, and chewy-edged, remove them from the smoker and serve with jasmine rice and some stir-fried bok choy and broccoli with a little finely chopped fresh red chile, if you want some heat.

SERVES 6

½ cup rice wine
½ cup dark soy sauce
½ cup light brown sugar
⅓ cup white wine vinegar
½ teaspoon sea salt
6 cardamom pods
2 ounces fresh ginger, peeled and sliced (about ½ cup)
½ cup ketchup
2¼ pounds beef ribs, cut into large chunks
jasmine rice and stir-fried bok choy and/or broccoli, to serve (optional)

MAPLE-SMOKED PORK RIBS

Maple wood works very nicely with pork and here the result is lovely, sweet and smoky ribs.

1 rack of pork ribs, weighing about 1¼ to 1½ pounds
2 tablespoons sea salt
2 tablespoons granulated or light brown sugar
2 tablespoons maple wood chips or shavings

First, prepare the ribs. Place them in a large, shallow Pyrex, glass, or ceramic dish and sprinkle with the salt and sugar. Rub all over the rack and transfer to the fridge for an hour.

Rinse and dry the ribs thoroughly on paper towels.

Set up your hot smoker, with maple chips sat on top of the charcoal. When the smoker is at the correct temperature, add the rack of ribs. Smoke for about an hour.

To finish off the ribs, roast them in a preheated oven at 350°F for 20 to 30 minutes until they are rich brown and sizzling. Serve hot.

For Maple smoked pork ribs with a brown sugar glaze, mix together ¼ cup of maple syrup and ¼ cup of light brown sugar to form a thick liquid. Follow the recipe as above, but as the ribs are smoking, brush them all over with glaze at 10 minute intervals throughout the process. This will give an extra, delicious, sweet and sticky glaze.

SPICED SMOKED LAMB SHOULDER

This is a wonderful way to prepare a shoulder of lamb, richly flavored with a dry spice rub. It is fantastic served with salads, couscous, and vegetable tagines.

Place the lamb in a large, shallow Pyrex, glass, or ceramic dish or bowl. Mix all the flavorings in a bowl and rub over the lamb. Cover the lamb with plastic wrap and transfer to the fridge for 6 hours.

When you are ready to smoke the lamb, preheat the hot smoker (see page 11). Place the lamb directly onto the rack and smoke for 1 to 2 hours, depending on how smoky you would like the lamb to taste.

To finish off the meat, you can either barbecue it for 1 hour, turning regularly, or roast it in a preheated oven at 325°F for 2 to 4 hours. Rest for 1 hour well wrapped in foil before shredding with two forks, and serving either hot or warm.

1 lamb shoulder, weighing about 5½ pounds
2½ tablespoons sea salt
¼ cup ground coriander seeds
2 tablespoons ground cumin
2 tablespoons chile powder—mild or hot
8 garlic gloves, crushed

LAMB SHAWARMA

Shawarma is a Middle Eastern wrap in which sliced or shredded meat is rolled in flatbread. Spicy smoked lamb is perfect for these. You can buy *khobez* flatbreads or pita bread but it's easy to make your own.

SERVES 6

FOR THE FLATBREADS
3 cups self-rising flour, plus extra for dusting
½ teaspoon sea salt
¾ cup warm water, mixed with ¼ cup olive oil

FOR THE SLAW
½ white cabbage, sliced very finely on
    a mandolin
zest and juice of 1 lemon
pinch of sea salt
½ cup fresh flat-leaf parsley, chopped
seeds of 1 pomegranate

FOR THE MINT YOGURT
¾ cup full-fat plain yogurt
½ cup fresh mint leaves, chopped
generous pinch of sea salt

1¼ pounds spiced, smoked, and cooked lamb
    shoulder meat (page 113), shredded—either
    warm or at room temperature

Start with the flatbread, if you are making your own. Mix all the ingredients together thoroughly in a large mixing bowl to form a soft ball of dough. Cover the bowl with plastic wrap and set aside for 20 minutes.

To cook, divide the dough evenly into 6 balls. Roll out each ball on a floured surface to form a circle about ¼-inch thick. Preheat a large nonstick frying pan over high heat until it's almost smoking, and then cook each flatbread one at a time in the dry pan for 2 to 3 minutes on each side.

To make the slaw, combine all the ingredients thoroughly in a bowl. Stir well and keep at room temperature.

To make the mint yogurt, stir the chopped mint into the yogurt and season with salt.

To serve, place the warm lamb and freshly cooked flatbreads on the table. Serve the slaw and mint yogurt in separate bowls and allow everyone to construct their own *shawarma* wrap. The individual components will keep for 24 hours if there are any leftovers.

SMOKED RABBIT

Rabbit is so delicious—lean and slightly sweet. It works best in slow-cooked dishes like casseroles, but the saddle or loin is lovely wrapped in smoked pancetta and pan-fried.

   As with any game, make sure you source your rabbit from a trusted supplier, so that the rabbit was healthy, of an appropriate age, and has been carefully raised.

2 teaspoons sea salt
2 large rabbits, broken down
olive oil

Rub the salt into the meat, then put it in a large, shallow Pyrex, glass, or ceramic dish, cover, and transfer to the fridge for 30 minutes to 2 hours.

Remove the meat from the fridge and rinse the sections of rabbit well under cold running water. Dry them thoroughly with paper towels and set aside ready to smoke.

Place the wood chips in the center of a hot smoker. When it is at the correct stage (see page 11), put the rabbit on the rack and smoke for 20 minutes. The meat should take on a more ocher shade and release some liquid.

Once the rabbit is smoked, it can be pan-fried briefly in a little olive oil to brown the pieces and put straight into a Dutch oven.

Alternatively, roast in the oven at 350°F for 15 to 20 minutes until the skin is crisp and the meat is fully cooked.

SMOKED RABBIT CASSEROLE

This is my smoky twist on a very simple, classic recipe for a rabbit casserole. It is nutritious and comforting served with buttery mashed potatoes and green vegetables.

2 large broken down rabbits, hot-smoked (see above)
2 tablespoons all-purpose flour
sea salt and freshly ground black pepper
2 tablespoons salted butter, plus extra (optional)
1 large white onion, thinly sliced
9 ounces smoked bacon (page 80), chopped into ½-inch pieces
1 tablespoon olive oil (optional)
1 large sprig of thyme
2 teaspoons Dijon mustard
2 cups cider
mashed potatoes and green vegetables or salad and crusty bread, to serve

Start by preparing the smoked rabbit. Put the pieces on a large plate, sprinkle with the flour, and season with salt and pepper. Ensure the rabbit pieces are lightly coated in flour on all sides. Set aside.

Select a large, flameproof, lidded Dutch oven—and melt the butter over medium heat. Add the rabbit pieces, shaking off any excess flour first, and cook for 5 to 10 minutes until golden brown. Don't increase the heat too much or the butter will burn. Remove the rabbit pieces from the pan and set aside on a plate.

Add the onion and bacon to the pan, keep the heat medium, and cook gently for about 10 minutes until they are fragrant and have softened a little. Do not allow the onions to color. If the pan is a little dry, add a tablespoon of olive oil or a little extra butter.

Return the rabbit pieces to the Dutch oven, followed by the remaining ingredients. Cover and simmer gently for 3 hours before serving with mashed potatoes and green vegetables or a salad and some good, crusty bread.

VEGETABLES & SALT

SMOKED CORN FRITTERS

Smoked corn is really delicious when stirred into a lightly spiced batter and made into fritters. This is an ideal recipe to make for a weekend brunch or lunch.

MAKES ABOUT 16 FRITTERS

1¼ cups self-rising flour
½ teaspoon sea salt
1 teaspoon ground cumin
1 teaspoon paprika
1 extra-large egg, beaten
2½ cups smoked corn kernels—
   about 2 to 3 cobs (page 122)
3 scallions, thinly sliced
2 tablespoons sunflower oil

Sift the flour, salt, cumin, and paprika into a large mixing bowl. Add the beaten egg and ½ cup water and whisk to form a thick batter. Stir in the corn and scallions. Set aside.

Add 1 tablespoon of oil to a large nonstick frying pan. Heat over medium to high heat. Swirl the pan to ensure the oil is evenly distributed over the bottom.

Preheat the oven to 220°F. Spoon 1 heaping tablespoon of mixture per fritter into the pan and cook for 2 to 3 minutes on each side until the fritters are rich brown. Work in batches and avoid overcrowding the pan. Transfer to a baking pan lined with parchment paper and keep warm in the oven until ready to serve.

Serve warm—they are excellent with an avocado salsa made from chopped avocado, tomato, fresh cilantro leaves, and lime juice.

SMOKED CORN ON THE COB

Smoked corn on the cob is delicious served buttered, or added to salads, burritos, tacos, crab cakes, and of course, the Smoked corn fritters on page 121.

SERVES 6

6 whole corn cobs, husks on or off

1½ teaspoons maple or mesquite wood chips

TIP

If you are smoking the corn with the husks off, rub a little neutral vegetable oil over the corn and season with a little salt and pepper before smoking.

Preheat your smoker with the wood chips inside. When the smoker is at about 200°F, add the corn and smoke for 30 minutes to 1 hour until the husks are as smoky as you like.

The smoked corn will keep in the fridge in an airtight container for up to 5 days. The kernels will stay fresher on the husk but you can strip them off the husks and store for ease of use, if you wish.

SMOKED BELL PEPPERS

Hot-smoked bell peppers work fantastically well in a myriad of recipes. Smoke them whole and then peel, chop, and seed the peppers as required. Red and green bell peppers are the most delicious and versatile peppers to smoke.

Preheat your smoker with the wood chips inside. When the smoker is at 200°F, add the whole bell peppers and smoke for 30 minutes to 1 hour until they are as smoky as you like.

Smoked peppers will keep, well wrapped, for up to 5 to 7 days in the fridge.

MAKES 4 SMOKED BELL PEPPERS

4 bell peppers

1½ teaspoons maple or mesquite wood chips

SMOKED RED BELL PEPPERS WITH CHORIZO AND SHERRY

This is an excellent dish to serve as part of a tapas spread. The smoky flavor comes from smoked red bell peppers and smoked paprika, or pimentón, in the chorizo. Use a traditional Spanish sherry and authentic cooking chorizo for the best flavor.

Heat the oil in a large frying pan and add the garlic. Cook for about 5 minutes until it smells fragrant and then add the chorizo. Cook for another 5 minutes over medium heat. You want the chorizo to start to release some of its fat, but don't let it burn.

Next, add the sliced smoked bell peppers, followed by a pinch of salt and the sherry. Cook gently for another 10 to 20 minutes until the chorizo is fully cooked. Stir in the parsley just before serving.

Serve warm in a bowl, with some good bread alongside for mopping up the delicious juices.

SERVES 4 AS A TAPAS

2 tablespoons extra virgin olive oil
1 garlic clove, finely chopped
5½ ounces spicy cooking chorizo, cut into ½-inch slices
4 smoked red bell peppers (see above), cut into ½-inch slices
pinch of sea salt
¼ cup amontillado sherry
1 heaping tablespoon chopped fresh flat-leaf parsley

SMOKED MUSHROOMS

Mushrooms respond to smoking very well and take on another layer of rich flavor. I think the brown varieties of mushroom are nicest smoked, as the smoke really enhances their deep, earthy flavor. Portobello and crimini are especially good, and hickory or chestnut woods are perfect partners.

Smoked mushrooms make an excellent addition to soups, risottos, salads, casseroles, and tarts.

Mushrooms can be cold smoked, but I prefer to hot smoke as it's a much quicker process—usually about 30 minutes from start to finish.

Makes 3 pounds

3 to 4 tablespoons olive oil
3 pounds brown mushrooms, such as Portobello or crimini
sea salt and freshly ground black pepper

1½ teaspoons hickory or chestnut wood chips

Gently brush or rub the olive oil over the surface of the mushrooms. Season with salt and pepper and set aside.

Preheat your smoker with the wood chips inside. When the smoker is at about 200°F, add the mushrooms and smoke for 20 to 50 minutes until the mushrooms are as smoky as you like. The amount of time you smoke the mushrooms for will vary depending on their size. I will often smoke them for a longer time so that they have started to soften and release liquid, and will be ready to eat as they are without further cooking.

The smoked mushrooms will keep in the fridge, in an airtight container, for up to 2 days.

PORK STROGANOFF WITH SMOKED MUSHROOMS

This is an excellent quick supper dish. A good stroganoff is creamy and warmly spiced. Smoked mushrooms add another layer of flavor. Hot-smoked large flat mushrooms are best here, as this dish allows their meaty texture to shine.

Serves 4

2 tablespoons salted butter
1¼-pound pork tenderloin, thinly sliced
1 large white onion, thinly sliced
8 ounces hot-smoked mushrooms (see above), thinly sliced
2 teaspoons paprika
⅔ cup heavy cream
sea salt and freshly ground black pepper
2 teaspoons lemon juice
2 teaspoons chopped fresh flat-leaf parsley
rice, to serve

Melt the butter in a large, nonstick frying pan. Add the sliced pork and gently stir-fry over medium heat for about 10 minutes until very lightly browned. Add the onion and cook for another 5 minutes then add the mushrooms. Cook for another 5 minutes, stirring regularly, before adding the paprika and cream. Allow the stroganoff to bubble away gently for 10 to 15 minutes.

Season well with salt and pepper; add the lemon juice and fresh parsley just before serving. Taste to check the seasoning and serve with rice.

SMOKED MUSHROOM RAGOÛT
WITH FRESH HERB POLENTA

This is my take on a northern Italian dish. It's rich, comforting, and with a depth of flavor that the smokiness of the mushrooms enhances. The mushrooms are so meaty this dish will appeal to non-vegetarians and vegetarians alike. Really good crusty bread and a well-dressed green salad, which can be as simple as watercress leaves tossed in extra virgin olive oil and lemon juice, are essential accompaniments—along with a good glass of red wine.

SERVES 4

FOR THE RAGOÛT

3 tablespoons salted butter

3 garlic cloves, coarsely chopped

1¾ pounds button mushrooms, thinly sliced

14 ounces smoked mushrooms (page 125), sliced (Portobello are good here)

4 sprigs fresh thyme

1 large sprig fresh rosemary

¾ cup red wine

½ cup heavy cream

sea salt and freshly ground black pepper

FOR THE POLENTA

3 tablespoons salted butter

1¾ cups whole milk

2 tablespoons fresh thyme leaves

1 tablespoon finely chopped fresh rosemary leaves

1¼ cups polenta or coarse cornmeal

½ cup Parmesan, grated, plus extra to serve

Start with the ragoût. Put the butter in a large pan and add the garlic. Melt the butter over low heat and gently cook the garlic for 3 to 5 minutes until fragrant. Add the button mushrooms in stages, about a third at a time, allowing each batch to cook down a little before adding the next round. This is simply to allow enough space in the pan. Add the smoked mushrooms once the button mushrooms have all been added to the pan.

When all the mushrooms are in the pan, add the thyme and rosemary. Stir and add the wine, cream, and season with salt and pepper. Cook for another 15 minutes.

Meanwhile, make the polenta. Put the butter and milk in a large frying pan. Warm gently and stir so that the butter melts. Add the herbs and polenta and gently stir over medium heat for about 5 minutes until the polenta thickens. Now, add the grated Parmesan and stir through. Taste to check the polenta is softened—it will retain a little crunch—and season to taste.

Serve the polenta immediately on a hot plate with the ragoût next to it, with a green salad and good bread, such as a baguette for mopping up any mushroom juices, and a scattering of Parmesan over the top if you wish.

TIP:

Don't serve with the mushrooms on the polenta if you're cooking for guests, as they will stain the polenta within seconds and it won't look as pretty.

SMOKED ONIONS

Smoked onions are a delicious and useful ingredient to have in the kitchen. Excellent in their own right, they are equally special added to soups, stews, and sauces and heavenly in the tart on page 130. You can also use shallots, but they will require less smoking time, as they will quickly become more intensely smoky.

Smoked onions will keep for about a week. Store them well wrapped in the fridge. However, they will also freeze well—if you have more than you require you can slice them and freeze them in bags then defrost and use as required.

To smoke the onions more quickly and to impart a fuller smoky flavor, cut the onions in half vertically, through the root with the skin on. For a more gentle flavor or a slower smoke, leave the onions whole—skins can be left on or removed; I prefer to leave them on. To halve the onions, cut them vertically (as opposed to around the equator) through the root with the skin on. There is no need to do any more to prepare your onions unless you would like to remove the skin.

If you have halved the onions, gently brush or rub the olive oil over the cut surface. Season with salt and pepper and set aside. Whole onions can be smoked as they are.

Preheat your hot smoker with the wood chips inside. When the smoker is at about 195°F, add the onions and smoke for 20 to 50 minutes until the onions are smoked to your liking. Start with a 20-minute smoke and experiment from there.

Store the onions in the fridge in an airtight container for up to 2 days before using.

MAKES 2 POUNDS SMOKED ONIONS

2 pounds onions (white, yellow, or red)
3 to 4 tablespoons olive oil, if onions are halved
sea salt and freshly ground pepper

1½ teaspoons hickory wood chips

SMOKED ONION TART WITH
SPINACH, BLUE CHEESE, AND SAGE

This tart is fantastically delicious and straightforward to make. The subtle smokiness of the onions pairs extremely well with the blue cheese. I have used Gorgonzola in this recipe as it has a wonderful mellow flavor and melts nicely, but do play around with your favorite and most local cheeses. This tart makes a super light lunch or appetizer.

SERVES 6

2 teaspoons olive oil
2 large hot-smoked white onions (page 129),
    cut into ¼-inch slices
2 garlic cloves, finely chopped
6 ounces spinach
13 ounces ready-rolled all-butter puff pastry
1¼ cups Gorgonzola dolce or soft blue cheese
½ cup Parmesan, finely grated
15 fresh sage leaves
1 large egg, beaten
crisp green salad, to serve

Preheat the oven to 400°F. Set aside a large, shallow, nonstick baking pan or sheet, at least 8 x 12 inches.

Heat the oil in a large nonstick frying pan over medium heat and cook the onion and garlic gently for about 10 minutes until smelling sweet and fragrant. They will look translucent and should not brown.

When the onions are softened, reduce the heat and stir in the spinach, stirring to encourage it to wilt gently.

Meanwhile, prepare the tart crust. Lay the pastry dough on the baking pan. Use a small, sharp knife to carefully score a border around the pastry dough, about ¾-inch from the edge.

Spoon the onion and spinach mixture carefully and evenly into the center of the dough, up to the scored borderline, but not right to the edge. Carefully dot chunks of Gorgonzola over the spinach and onions, followed by the Parmesan and sage leaves.

Finish by carefully brushing the beaten egg over the exposed pastry border; this will give it a wonderful shine and rich brown color.

Bake the tart for 20 to 30 minutes until the topping is bubbling and golden brown, and the crust has puffed and is a rich brown color. Serve warm or cold with a crisp green salad.

SMOKED GARLIC

Garlic can be hot or cold smoked but hot-smoked garlic is preferable because the flavor penetrates the cloves better.

Try using your smoked garlic in homemade garlic butter, stuffing a whole bulb in a chicken before roasting, or adding it to risottos or pasta sauces.

Preheat your smoker with the wood chips inside. When the smoker is at 195°F, add the whole garlic bulbs and smoke for 20 to 50 minutes until the bulbs are smoked to your liking.

Store the garlic in the fridge in an airtight container for up to 2 days before using. The smoked garlic will keep in the fridge for at least 2 weeks in an airtight container.

MAKES 4 BULBS

4 bulbs fresh garlic, unpeeled

1½ teaspoons hickory wood chips

SMOKED GARLIC DAUPHINOISE POTATOES

This is the very best recipe for Dauphinoise potatoes I've made and everyone seems to love it. Smoked garlic adds a subtle yet delectable layer of umami. Try it.

Serves 6 to 8

butter, for greasing
2¼ pounds large Russet potatoes, peeled
1¾ cups heavy cream
3 smoked garlic cloves (page 134), peeled and very finely chopped
salt and freshly ground black pepper
1¾ cups Cheddar, grated

Preheat the oven to 400°F. Butter a large ovenproof dish—I use a shallow rectangular ceramic dish, measuring 8 x 12 inches. Set aside.

Slice the potatoes into ⅛-inch thick slices using a mandolin. Rinse the slices well in cold water until the water runs clear, and dry each slice thoroughly using a clean kitchen towel. This takes time, but removing the excess starch from the potatoes makes a real difference to the end result.

Pour the cream into a saucepan and gently warm until it just shivers, and remove from the heat.

Place a layer of potato slices to cover the bottom of the buttered dish, sprinkle with a few flecks of chopped smoked garlic, and season generously with salt and pepper. Repeat, forming layers of potato and garlic, remembering to season each layer as you go. Finally, pour the warmed cream over the potatoes and sprinkle the grated cheese evenly over the top. Bake for 25 to 35 minutes until the top is a rich brown color and the cream is bubbling. Stick a sharp knife into the potatoes, to test they are fully tender—you should meet no resistance. If the potatoes are a little firm but the top is brown, cover the dish with foil and bake for another 10 minutes before testing again. Cut into portions using a sharp knife and serve hot.

SMOKED CHILES

Smoked fresh chiles have a really interesting flavor and are a subtle and delicious way of imparting a little smoke into your cooking.

Preheat your smoker with the wood chips inside. When the smoker is at 195°F, add the chiles and smoke for 15 to 45 minutes until they are as smoky as you like.

Smoked chiles will keep, well wrapped, for up to 7 days in the fridge.

MAKES 8 SMOKED CHILES

8 fresh chiles of your choice, from the little bird's eye to Scotch bonnet

1½ teaspoons wood chips (see page 12 for suggestions to pair with vegetables)

SMOKED CHILLI CON CARNE

Smoked chiles add a fantastic layer of flavor to this rich, dark chilli con carne. The flavors improve with a long, slow simmer throughout the day.

Put half the oil in a large frying pan, set over medium heat, and add the onions. Cook for about 15 minutes over medium heat until they are fragrant and translucent. Remove and set aside on a plate.

Return the pan to the heat, add the remaining oil, increase the heat to high, and cook the beef until it is lightly browned. When the meat is browned, add the beans, chiles, vinegar, and sugar and stir through the meat.

Transfer to a large saucepan, Dutch oven, or a slow cooker, and add the onions and the remaining ingredients. Stir well, cover, and leave to simmer away very gently, stirring occasionally, for at least 3 hours until the sauce is rich and thick. (It will take about the same time in a slow cooker.) Serve hot with rice or baked sweet potatoes.

SERVES 6 TO 8

4 tablespoons olive oil
2 large white onions, finely chopped
1¼ pounds ground beef
1 x 14-ounce can black beans, drained and rinsed
3 red or green smoked chiles (see above)
2 tablespoons cider vinegar
2 tablespoons dark brown sugar
2 x 14-ounce cans chopped tomatoes
1 cup beef stock
1 cinnamon stick
2 bay leaves
1 large sprig fresh thyme
1 to 3 teaspoons chile powder according to taste
sea salt and freshly ground black pepper
rice or baked sweet potatoes, to serve

SMOKED SEA SALT

MAKES ⅓ CUP

⅓ cup sea salt crystals

a wooden plank, soaked in water for at least 2 hours

TIP:

You can also use the planks to smoke other ingredients, such as chicken or duck breasts, and even to smoke hard or semi-soft cheeses.

It is easy to buy a good smoked sea salt, but it is really fun to try making your own. You will need some wood planks that are specially designed for smoking food—oak or cedar work well.

Smoke as much or as little salt as you like in one shot—the smoke time will be the same.

Set the hot smoker and place the plank on the rack inside. Pour the salt carefully onto the plank and smoke for 30 minutes to 1 hour. It will turn a rich amber color as it smokes. Remove from the smoker and let cool before storing in an airtight container.

Use in sweet and savory recipes, as you would standard sea salt. It is especially good sprinkled on barbecued meats.

SMOKED SEA SALT CARAMEL

Salted caramel is a wonderful thing. It is a very useful ingredient, both as a spread and as a thick sauce for spooning onto desserts and ice cream. I like to add smoked sea salt to caramel for another layer of complexity.

MAKES ABOUT 1 PINT

1½ cups superfine sugar
⅔ cup heavy cream
3 tablespoons salted butter
½ teaspoon smoked sea salt (see above)

Put the sugar and ½ cup cold water in a large pan. Stir occasionally and gently warm the sugar. When it has dissolved, increase the heat to high and boil without stirring until the caramel turns a deep, rich brown.

Once the caramel is a deep, rich brown color, remove the pan from the heat. You may wish to cover your hand with an oven mitt and step back a little as you pour in the cream. Add the butter and the salt and stir to form a thick, smooth caramel.

The caramel can splatter, so do be careful.

Set the caramel aside to cool. It is wonderful served over ice cream or as a pouring sauce with desserts, stirred into brownie mixture, spooned onto cookies, or drizzled over chocolate mousse. It will store well in the fridge for up to a month, kept in a sealed, sterilized container.

SMOKED SEA SALT TRUFFLES

These truffles make a really lovely present and are delicious served with coffee after dinner. They have a very soft caramel-like texture, and the smoked sea salt gives a subtle surprise at the end. The combination of salt and smoke works so well with chocolate.

Put the cream and sugar in a medium-sized saucepan. Heat gently and simmer for 1 minute. Chop the chocolate into small pieces in a small bowl. Pour the cream onto the chocolate and whisk well to form a glossy ganache. Gently stir in the sea salt. Cool the ganache and refrigerate for 2 hours.

Roll the truffles into balls about ¾-inch in diameter and dust them in sifted cocoa powder. These truffles will keep in an airtight container for up to 1 week.

MAKES 50 TRUFFLES

1½ cups heavy cream
½ cup superfine sugar
10½ ounces dark chocolate (62 to 70 percent cocoa solids)
1 level teaspoon smoked sea salt (page 138)
½ cup cocoa powder, for rolling

INDEX

A
Abu Garcia smokers 8
almonds
  smoked *merguez* salad with orange, watercress, and honey spiced almonds 105
Asian smoked mackerel salad 34
Asian-spiced hot-smoked salmon 25
Asian-spiced smoked beef ribs 111

B
bacon
  drying 7
  salted 6
  smoked
    feijoada 108
    homemade 80
    maple and brown sugar cured 80
    smoked rabbit casserole 117
  smoked bacon jam with maple and whiskey 83
  smoked scallop salad with bacon and Puy lentils 56
barbecued lobster with smoked butter 74
barbecues, lidded 8
beans
  feijoada 108
beef
  Asian-spiced smoked beef ribs 111
  braised smoked beef cheeks with gremolata 107
  smoked beef cheeks 107
  smoked beef ribs 111
  smoked chilli con carne 137
Big Green Eggs 8, 9
bread
  flatbreads 114
  hot-smoked trout pâté with sourdough toasts 53
  rye 31
  smoked cod's roe *skagen* 59
  whole-wheat 19
brining 6-7, 16, 49
butter
  smoked 6, 74
    barbecued lobster with smoked butter 74
    smoked butter fudge 77
butternut squash
  orecchiette baked with squash, smoked ricotta, and sage 72

C
cabbage
  lamb *shawarma* 114
Camerons stovetop smokers 8
capers
  celeriac and caper remoulade 41
  hot-smoked trout pâté with sourdough toasts 53
caramel, smoked sea salt 138
celeriac and caper remoulade 41
charcoal 9, 12 13
cheese 6

rygeost 69
smoked Cheddar 62
  smoked Cheddar, mushroom, and leek tart 65
smoked ham hock croquetas 98
smoked mozzarella 62
  melanzane parmigiana with smoked mozzarella 66
smoked onion tart with spinach, blue cheese, and sage 130
smoked ricotta 62
  orecchiette baked with squash, smoked ricotta, and sage 72
smoked Roquefort 68
  smoked blue cheese salad with pears and walnuts 68
Swiss chalet potatoes 91
chicken
  smoked chicken breast 85
  smoked chicken and chorizo paella 89
  smoked chicken salad with mango, chile, and fresh herbs 90
chiles
  smoked 137
  smoked chicken salad with mango, chile, and fresh herbs 90
  smoked chilli con carne 137
chocolate
  smoked sea salt truffles 141
chorizo
  feijoada 108
  smoked chicken and chorizo paella 89
  smoked red bell peppers with chorizo and sherry 123
cod roe
  smoked 58
  smoked cod's roe *skagen* 59
  taramasalata 58
cold smokers 8 9
  building 9 11
cold smoking 4, 5, 11 12
corn
  smoked corn on the cob 122
  smoked corn fritters 120
cross contamination, avoiding 12
cucumber, pickled 20
curing 6

D
dry curing 7
drying 7
duck
  hot-smoked duck breasts 84
  smoked duck salad with orange, pomegranate, and pecans 86

E
eggplant
  melanzane parmigiana with smoked mozzarella 66
eggs
  kippers Florentine 46
equipment 8 11

F
fennel salad 41
fish
  curing and salting 6

flatbreads
  lamb *shawarma* 114
fritters
  smoked corn fritters 120
fudge, smoked butter 77

G
garlic
  braised smoked beef cheeks with gremolata 107
  smoked 133
    smoked garlic dauphinoise potatoes 134
grouse, smoked 85

H
haddock, hot-smoked 32
  Scandinavian fiskefrikadeller 41
  smoked haddock mousse with lemon hollandaise and shrimp 36
  smoked haddock and shrimp fish pie 38
ham
  smoked ham hock 94
  smoked ham hock croquetas 98
  spice glazed smoked ham 92
hardwood 5, 9, 11
health and safety 10
herbs in marinades 7
herring
  herring, potato, and watercress salad 45
  hot smoked herring fillets 42
history of smoking 4
hot dog buns 100
hot dogs (*pølse*) 100
hot smokers 8
  outdoor 11
  stovetop 8, 11, 13
hot smoking 4 5, 11

K
kielbasa 103
kippers 42
  kippers Florentine 46
  traditional 45

L
lamb
  lamb *shawarma* 114
  spiced smoked lamb shoulder 113
leeks
  trout with leeks, *rygeost*, and dill 71
  smoked Cheddar, mushroom, and leek tart 65
lentils
  smoked scallop salad with bacon and Puy lentils 56
lobster
  barbecued lobster with smoked butter 74

M
mackerel
  hot smoked 32
  Asian smoked mackerel salad 34
mangoes
  Asian smoked mackerel salad 34
  smoked chicken salad with mango, chile, and fresh herbs 90
maple syrup
  maple and brown sugar cured bacon 80

maple smoked pork ribs with a brown
  sugar glaze 112
smoked bacon jam with maple and
  whiskey 83
maple smoked pork ribs 112
marinades 7
materials for smoking 5, 9, 12
meat
  brining 6-7
  curing 6
  salting 6
monkfish
  hot-smoked 55
  smoked monkfish with prosciutto and
    rosemary 55
mushrooms
  smoked 125
    pork stroganoff with smoked
      mushrooms 125
    smoked mushroom ragoût with fresh
      herb polenta 126
    smoked Cheddar, mushroom, and leek tart
      65
mustard
  mustard and dill sauce 20
  smoked rabbit casserole 117
  spice glazed smoked ham 92

O

onions
  ristede løg 100
  smoked 129
    smoked onion tart with spinach, blue
      cheese, and sage 130
oranges
  smoked duck salad with orange,
    pomegranate, and pecans 86
  smoked *merguez* salad with orange,
    watercress, and honey spiced almonds 105
outdoor hot smokers 11

P

partridge, smoked 85
pasta
  fresh tagliatelle with smoked trout and
    watercress 50
  orecchiette baked with squash, smoked
    ricotta, and sage 72
peaches
  smoked shrimp, peach, and mint salad 28
peanuts
  Asian smoked mackerel salad 34
pears
  smoked roquefort salad with pears and
    walnuts 68
pecans
  smoked duck salad with orange,
    pomegranate, and pecans 86
pellicle 6
peppers, bell
  smoked 123
    smoked red bell peppers with chorizo
      and sherry 123
pheasant, smoked 85
polenta
  smoked mushroom ragoût with fresh herb
    polenta 126

pølse 100
pomegranates
  lamb *shawarma* 114
  smoked duck salad with orange,
    pomegranate, and pecans 86
pork
  feijoada 108
  kielbasa 103
  maple smoked pork ribs 112
  pork stroganoff with smoked mushrooms
    125
  smoked pork belly 108
potatoes
  herring, potato, and watercress salad 45
  Scandinavian fiskefrikadeller 41
  smoked garlic dauphinoise potatoes 134
  smoked haddock and shrimp fish pie 38
  Swiss chalet potatoes 91
presmoking 6
prosciutto
  smoked monkfish with prosciutto and
    rosemary 55

R

rabbit
  smoked 117
  smoked rabbit casserole 117
rice
  smoked chicken and chorizo paella 89
ricotta, smoked 62
  orecchiette baked with squash, smoked
    ricotta, and sage 72
rillettes, smoked salmon 22
ristede løg 100
rosemary
  smoked monkfish with prosciutto and
    rosemary 55
rubs 7
rye bread 31
rygeost 69
  fresh trout with leeks, *rygeost*, and dill 71

S

sage
  orecchiette baked with squash, smoked
    ricotta, and sage 72
  smoked onion tart with spinach, blue
    cheese, and sage 130
salmon
  brining 6-7
  cold smoked 16
  drying 7
    with mustard and dill sauce, pickles, and
      whole-wheat bread 18-21
  hot-smoked 23
    Asian-spiced hot-smoked salmon 25
    smoked salmon rillettes 22
salting 6
sausages, smoked 6, 99
  kielbasa 103
  merguez 102, 105
  pølse 100
scallops
  hot-smoked 56
    smoked scallop salad with bacon and Puy
      lentils 56
scamorza 62
Scandinavian fiskefrikadeller 41

sea salt 6
  smoked 138
  smoked sea salt caramel 138
  smoked sea salt truffles 141
shallots, smoked 129
shrimp
  hot-smoked 26
    skagenröra 31
    smoked shrimp, peach, and mint salad
      28
    smoked haddock mousse with lemon
      hollandaise and shrimp 36
    smoked haddock and shrimp fish pie 38
skagenröra 31
smoking mixes 5
smoking process 11-13
  charcoal 9, 12-13
  cold smoking 4, 5, 11-12
  filling the smoker 12
  hot smoking 4 5, 11
  lighting the fire 10, 13
  materials for smoking 5, 9, 12
  soaking chips 12
  where to smoke 13
spice glazed smoked ham 92
spiced smoked lamb shoulder 113
spices in marinades 7
spinach
  kippers Florentine 46
  smoked onion tart with spinach, blue
    cheese, and sage 130
stovetop hot smokers 8, 11, 13
Swiss chalet potatoes 91

T

taramasalata 58
thermometers 7
tomatoes
  orecchiette baked with squash, smoked
    ricotta, and sage 72
trout
  cold-smoked 49
    fresh tagliatelle with smoked trout and
      watercress 50
    trout with leeks, *rygeost*, and dill 71
  hot-smoked 48
    pâté with sourdough toasts 53

W

walnuts
  caramelized 68
  smoked roquefort salad with pears and
    walnuts 68
watercress
  fresh tagliatelle with smoked trout and
    watercress 50
  herring, potato, and watercress salad 45
  smoked *merguez* salad with orange
    watercress, and honey spiced almonds 105
whiskey
  smoked bacon jam with maple and
    whiskey 83
whole-wheat bread 19
wood for smoking 5, 9, 12

Y

yogurt
  lamb *shawarma* 114

SUPPLIERS

Ingredients and good-quality equipment are everything.

Usually the best place to find high-quality ingredients is your local farmer's market. Try to talk directly to the farmers and tell them what type of meat, dairy, or produce you're seeking.

For sustainably raised and hard-to-find meats, here are some recommended sources:
www.belcampo.com
www.dartagnan.com
www.heritagefoodsusa.com
www.hudsonvalleyfoiegras.com
www.slagelfamilyfarm.com
www.whiteoakpastures.com

For specialty seafood items:
www.petrossian.com

For smokers and accessories:
www.bradleysmoker.com
www.cabelas.com
www.cookshack.com
www.fieldandstreamshop.com
www.gandermountain.com
www.homedepot.com
www.lowes.com
www.williams-sonoma.com

Also, try your local hardware store, which may be able to order smokers if not in regular stock.

ACKNOWLEDGMENTS

First of all, thanks to you for buying this book. Writing cookbooks is my dream job, but it is nothing without my readers. Thank you to you all for reading my work, and to every one of you who takes the time to write and tell me how much you and your families love my recipes. It means so much to me.

Sincerest thanks to Kyle for asking me to write this book and for your support. I have absolutely loved writing this one. Thank you to my brilliant editor Vicky for being so helpful, relaxed, and supportive at every step of the way. Indeed, my thanks are extended to the whole team at Kyle Books. It is a pleasure to work with you all. Thank you for your hard work on my behalf.

As ever, my brilliant agent Clare has been completely amazing. I can't thank you enough for all your help and support.

It has been such a great pleasure and privilege to work with my creative dream team to make this book come to life. Tara's photos, Annie's styling, ably assisted by Lola, and Tab's props all bring my recipes to life and make them look better than I had dreamt of. Thank you to you all for being such a pleasure to work with, and for the great care, attention, dedication, and passion you put into my work.

Writing a book involves a lot of hard work and I could not have managed without having Louise by my side, as with every one of my books, thanks for all your practical help on recipe test days and for being the best kitchen companion I could wish for. Thank you to all my other assistants, especially Kerri Fiona-Brookes, Alexandra Wilby, Charlotte Harvey, and Wendy Sharpe for being so wonderfully obliging and diligent and such a joy to work with, too.

Sincerest thanks to my suppliers—Big Green Egg, Piper's Farm, and Riverford—for getting behind this book from the very beginning. I really appreciate your assistance.

Thanks a million to my supporters, Mitsubishi Motors in the UK, for all your support. It is a pleasure to work with you and thank you for providing me with my amazing Outlander PHEV which has allowed me to get out and about smoking all over the country.

Many thanks to Rachel Allen for your support.

I owe a huge debt of gratitude to my parents for everything you do for me. I really do appreciate it all. Thank you very, very much. Hugest thanks also to Lucy and Andy. You do so much for me too, and I am so grateful for it all.

Thank you to Jean and Tony for everything you do to help me and for looking after me so well on weekends—even when we show up very late and unannounced!

As ever, thank you to my truly wonderful friends for being so understanding and tolerant—especially when my very heavy workload means that I have to change our plans or can't go out very often. I hope you all know your friendship means the world to me.

And finally, thank you to Tony for your constant support, encouragement, and love.